Published in Great Britain, 2008
by **The Howard League for Penal Reform**
1 Ardleigh Road, London N1 4HS
www.howardleague.org

ISBN 978-1-905994-06-9

CONTENTS

Foreword

Last year saw the centenary of the probation service. Sadly what was once a powerful institution for good has been undermined by the creation of the National Offender Management Service (NOMS) and its target driven culture. In January 2008, a restructuring of NOMS then saw the probation and prison services merged. From the chief executive down to area management, the 'winner' of this merger has undoubtedly been the prison service and its emphasis on centralised accountability. If the message being sent out appears questionable – that the balance between custodial and community solutions is weighted in favour of the jailers – it only reflects the lack of vision coming from government. Panicked exhortations from ministers to the courts not to send more people to overstuffed jails means nothing without a coherent strategy that recognises the complexity and variety of offending behaviour and appropriate community-based responses to this. As a result, an emphasis on monitoring offenders in the community has taken precedence over provision of guidance or direction on housing, social services and other needs.

We are all aware of the massive strains of overcrowding on the prison service but what receives less attention is the equally serious overcrowding that afflicts probation. Probation officers face ever-mounting caseloads without the resources to always meet demand. If there is to be any benefit from prisons and probation being brought together, it is that the common pressures between the two are properly acknowledged and service delivery is co-ordinated to improve affairs.

The Howard League for Penal Reform has conducted research (The Howard League for Penal Reform 2007) demonstrating that community sentences can reduce reoffending by up to 22% compared with short custodial sentences of up to 12 months. But while community sentences can be much more effective than short spells in prison, they are all too often poorly resourced and lack real political backing from the government. The result is a dearth of public confidence in community-based solutions to crime.

The Community Sentences Handbook we have now published seeks to highlight where good practice is occurring around the country, in some ways against the institutional odds. It also highlights what is needed to make community sentences perform more effectively – from unpaid work to restorative justice interventions. All too often, pockets of good practice flourish independently, for brief periods, but there is not the continuity or indeed co-ordination, that should be expected.

This handbook concentrates on practice and 'on the ground' solutions. More broadly, what is required is a restructured and properly resourced probation service, a new organisation focused on delivering locally tailored solutions to a national standard. Bringing prisons and probation together, as the government has, is not the answer. The probation service needs its own fresh identity, indeed a champion should be appointed who can be the public face of community sentences – an individual accountable for the success or failure of the system, building up trust and public confidence in community-based solutions.

The new organisation, which we have suggested should be renamed the Resolution Service, would work with both offenders and victims of crime. The positive reactions to restorative justice programmes from victims highlight how the solutions to crime are not simply about punishing, or indeed rehabilitating, the offender. It is also about engaging with victims to bring them resolution and we believe that restorative justice paves the way forward.

The Resolution Service would provide the national structure but there must be a local emphasis to the delivery of community sentences, also seeking to engage with more than simply those who commit crime. We suggest that community panels are established to consult local people about community sentences and, in particular, about unpaid work by offenders. Strong local links and local accountability are vital if community sentences are to meet the needs of people who offend and successfully prevent reoffending.

Robust, properly resourced community sentences that demonstrably cut reoffending rates will best serve the interests of public protection in the long term. If faith is placed in community sentencing, then the reduction in prison numbers will also allow far more productive work to be done in areas such as education and training for those individuals that must be held in custody. The alternative of an ever-rising prison population is simply unsustainable and will do nothing to make people feel safer. However long it takes, this is the truth that our society slowly works towards.

The Howard League for Penal Reform is grateful to the Esmée Fairbairn Foundation and their Rethinking Crime and Punishment initiative for funding the Community Programmes Awards, which formed the basis for this handbook. I would also take this opportunity to thank our judges for all their work on the Awards.

Frances Crook
Director, the Howard League for Penal Reform

Introduction

This Community Sentences Handbook brings together the lessons from the first two years of the Howard League for Penal Reform's Community Programmes Awards, part of the Community Sentences Cut Crime campaign.

The competition, a joint initiative between the Howard League for Penal Reform and the Esmée Fairbairn Foundation, was launched in November 2005 as part of the Howard League for Penal Reform's aim of encouraging public and government support for community sentences. We believe that well-resourced and well-structured programmes will raise public protection, bringing down the rate of reoffending, and repay the damage done by crime in a way which custodial sentences cannot.

By finding outstanding community programmes that work with individuals who have committed crime, it was hoped that the Community Programmes Awards would not only celebrate success but also promote positive practice in the delivery of community sentences. There have been three rounds of winners announced thus far - in 2005, 2006 and 2007 - with 27 schemes across the UK receiving awards.

The competition was open to statutory agencies and voluntary organisations, which were developing innovative community schemes. The programmes nominated were required to show some, but not all, of the following criteria:

- are part of a community sentence;
- are rehabilitative and help to prevent future offending;
- are realistic and positive;
- recognise the individual circumstances of offenders;
- offer a programme tailored to individual needs;
- meet the needs of specific client groups, for example, women, young people or ethnic minorities;
- involve users in planning and evaluation;
- are based on restorative principles;
- encourage offenders to think about the consequences of their crime;
- are cost effective;
- encourage offenders into employment or education; or
- work collaboratively with the local community.

A judging panel, which I chaired, was convened, comprising leading figures in the criminal justice sector and this team considered all nominations to the competition. There were two types of award available: Schemes of Special Merit for particularly exceptional programmes that caught the judges' attention and an Outstanding Schemes award for other community programmes of excellence that deserved recognition.

I said earlier that the Awards, and this handbook, celebrate and promote positive practice. There is an important point of discrimination to make here, as this is not a handbook of best practice. While all the projects covered in this handbook are deserved winners, many of the programmes featured had gaps in delivery and room for improvement. Some of the projects, for example, do not have any evaluation of their work in place; others don't mention or collate vital data such as reoffending figures;

hardly any of the projects mentioned costs. In short, the competition was not an exercise in backslapping. For all the positive practice we found, there were also notable failings to take into account.

Perhaps the most common failing we encountered was poor communication. Otherwise excellent projects let themselves down by being weak at communicating what exactly it was they did, how they did it and why they were successful. This included sharing information with other community programmes. It is particularly galling, given the shaky public confidence in community sentencing, to see successful programmes that are unable to get across the good they are doing. On occasion, there were great stories hidden away but the programmes lacked the 'good news sense' to identify them. At times, even this handbook suffers from descriptive gaps because of patchy information from the programmes themselves.

Having said that, the Community Sentences Handbook does provide us with an opportunity to rectify something of the weakness in communication. In the pages that follow, policy makers and practitioners alike can find out exactly what community programmes up and down the country can learn from each other.

At a time of great change in social and penal policy, we hope that some of the ideas and practices we describe can help inform practice at a local and national level. We can all learn from each other.

Professor David Wilson
Vice Chair, the Howard League for Penal Reform

CHAPTER 1

Contributions From Members of the Judging Panel

The Importance of Community Programmes

Lord Carter's report Securing the Future (Carter 2007) has ignited a much needed debate about how best to deal with offenders in England and Wales. His controversial proposals for a multi-billion pound prison building programme provide an opportunity for practitioners, voluntary organisations and others concerned with penal policy to come up with a much needed alternative vision; one which offers a better chance of rehabilitating offenders at much less of a financial, social and ethical cost.

One central plank to such an approach must be the provision of high-quality community-based programmes which provide police, prosecutors, courts and the Parole Board with effective options for responding to young and adult offenders. At their best, such programmes – whether run by probation services, youth offending teams (YOTs) or non-governmental organisations – can form a key part of a comprehensive approach to crime which enjoys the support and involvement of local agencies and residents. They can enable people in conflict with the law to make amends for the harm they have caused, to address the personal, social and health problems which lie behind their offending and to develop the determination and skills they need to lead a law abiding life.

Recognising, encouraging and publicising the best examples of such programmes, through the Howard League for Penal Reform's annual award scheme, plays an important role in tackling the crisis of confidence which has threatened to engulf community supervision in recent years.

Three elements of community programmes deserve particular attention at the present time. The first is the extent to which they can succeed in involving local people, civil society groups and statutory organisations in the wide range of activities through which offenders pay their debt to society and seek to put their past behind them. Research for Rethinking Crime and Punishment (2004) found that two-thirds of the public were interested in having a say about what forms of unpaid community work they would like offenders to do and there is encouraging evidence that this is now happening – a third of unpaid work projects are nominated by the public in some way. But there is still considerable scope for a more deep-seated and longer-term partnership between criminal justice agencies on the one hand and community groups on the other.

This will require public, private and voluntary organisations, particularly local authorities to get involved much more systematically with the community supervision of offenders. People who go to prison are predominantly drawn from the most deprived neighbourhoods and local authorities are well placed to co-ordinate the provision of housing, education, work and healthcare which are key to their rehabilitation. Evidence from the Local Government Association suggests that local authority involvement is still relatively patchy. A recent survey has found that local authorities have more staff with responsibility for reducing reoffending and are working more closely with other agencies (including the police and probation services) than in the past. Almost all local authorities seem to have at least one local strategy which covers reducing reoffending and more of them rate it as a high priority than previously. Relationships with the Crown Court, magistrates' courts and the prison service seem to be less positive however.

There is a strong case for developing more practical programmes such as multi-agency 'adult offending teams' along the lines of those developed in youth justice, local authorities taking a lead role in resettlement of short-term prisoners, or the expansion of neighbourhood justice centres based in areas with highest concentrations of need.

The second key element in community supervision is the largely untapped opportunity which it provides for offering restorative justice (RJ) options. In its purest form RJ involves victims and offenders meeting face-to-face in the presence of a facilitator, but a wide range of approaches have been developed which encourage offenders to take responsibility for the harm they have caused and for taking steps to put things right. A recent review of the UK and international evidence has concluded that RJ provides more satisfaction for both victims and offenders than does conventional criminal justice, helps victims get over their experience, and reduces repeat offending for some offenders. Despite this, RJ still hovers at the margins of our justice system. Despite its proven value, RJ is available only in parts of the youth justice system and its potential has not been exploited for strengthening local communities and developing neighbourhood policing. It is almost entirely absent in adult criminal justice where it could be very effective in reducing the need for prison whilst also tackling reoffending. Excellent experimental initiatives such as RJ conferencing for robbery and burglary in London fail to get mainstreamed because no one agency has responsibility for delivering RJ or for training staff and monitoring impact.

The third element of community programmes is the way that they are seen by the public and used by the courts. Various efforts have been made to increase public awareness about the range of non-custodial options, with mixed results. About two-thirds of people claim to be aware of community sentences but the percentage of people saying they know a great deal or a fair amount about community sentencing has decreased from 33% in 2005 to 29% in 2007. More people now believe that community sentences provide a tough punishment for adult offenders and are an effective means of punishing someone – but more also believe that community sentences are easier than prison.

There is almost no evidence about whether initiatives to boost public confidence have influenced sentencing practice. Previous research has shown that even measures specifically designed to increase the confidence of sentencers have not led to reductions in the use of custody but rather increased the imposition of requirements on community orders (see glossary). There is no guarantee that boosting the confidence of sentencers in community sentences will lead them to impose them *instead of prison*. It could result in such orders being imposed for lower tariff cases – in place of discharges or fines rather than prison sentences (if offenders then breach the orders and go to prison, the net result may even be an increase in imprisonment). The Carter review suggests that this has, in fact, been happening over the last ten years, during which time the number of community penalties imposed at all courts rose from 130,000 in 1995 to 191,000 in 2006 – an increase of 47%.

The challenge now is, therefore, to ensure that community supervision programmes work well for both offenders and victims and that they involve the wider community. Steps must be taken to ensure that community penalties are used as far as possible to displace prison sentences as part of a broader strategy of using prison much more sparingly than in recent years.

Rob Allen, Director, International Centre for Prison Studies, Co-ordinator, Rethinking Crime and Punishment, Implementing the Findings

Opportunities Presented by Community Programmes for Greater Involvement in the Delivery of Effective Services to Offenders

If you want to have a few minutes of harmless fun, try entering the phrase 'walks free' into an Internet search engine. You'll get plenty of returns from the UK tabloid press. Such-and-such an offender, who has received a six-month suspended prison sentence and 100 hours community service, 'walks free' from court. I can't be the only one who is wound up by the frequency with which this phrase features in the headline of an article about a case where the offender receives a community order. It seems that we still have a long way to go to persuade at least large sections of the print media that there is any punishment of real value other than prison.

But it does not have to be this way. There are credible alternatives in the community and we should not be afraid to sing the praises of those who work hard to make them effective. When the new community order became available to the courts in England and Wales in April 2005, it brought together all the existing community sentences for adults into one flexible sentence. There are 12 separate requirements from which sentencers can pick and mix to tailor the sentence they hand down to the seriousness of the offence and the needs and characteristics of the offender in front of them.

This sentence served in the community provides greater scope for requiring offenders to address the factors which have influenced their offending than does a short time in prison. A man who hits his partner can be ordered to attend a programme specifically designed to challenge the attitudes behind this and to provide skills to enable him to behave differently – witness the Sacro scheme in Scotland, which won a Howard League for Penal Reform Community Programmes Award. These programmes have been accredited by experts as following principles which evidence shows are most likely to be successful in reducing the risk of reoffending. Drug and alcohol requirements are available to confront those for whom these substances either fuel or motivate offending.

The best evidence we have says that when such intervention takes place in the community and the offender engages with it, it is more likely to be successful than a similar intervention delivered in prison.

For many offenders, being challenged to deal with difficult issues in their lives linked to their offending is tougher than spending a few weeks locked up. Indeed, many offenders are released from a short prison sentence without doing anything at all to reduce their risk of reoffending. For many persistent minor offenders, prison does nothing other than momentarily interrupt their behaviour. It may even make the chances of them reoffending further even higher.

A curfew requirement backed by an electronic tag can also have a role in supporting offenders in completing other requirements placed on them by the court, providing, as it does, a measure of restriction on them which can help to bring order into an otherwise chaotic life.

Offenders can be required, as part of a community order, to do work to benefit the community. Community Payback (see glossary) is a way of making this more visible to society – communities have the opportunity to choose what the work should be and the sites where the work is completed have signs advertising the fact that it is being done by offenders as part of their sentence.

Where the court's focus is on punishing the offender (as opposed to trying to stop them from reoffending), another weapon in its armoury is the curfew as a stand-alone requirement. The court can 'ground' an offender overnight and be confident that, if the offender leaves the designated location, this will be notified to the contractors who enforce the sentence.

The National Probation Service (NPS) is now more effective than ever at ensuring that offenders actually do what the court requires. And where offenders slip up – whether in a big or small way – probation officers take action to ensure that the courts are able to enforce the orders or re-sentence the offender before too long.

So, community sentences can make a significant contribution to the punishment of offenders in England and Wales and I applaud the Howard League for Penal Reform for its work in promoting local schemes which are particularly innovative and effective in achieving this, and I've been pleased to be part of the judging panel for the award scheme. But what can we do to make it easier for courts to have the confidence to use them more readily instead of prison?

For a start, we need to do all we can to discourage use of the kind of language which implies that someone who receives a community sentence has got off lightly. For those who do not need to be locked up, it is an effective and versatile punishment. We must be bolder in proclaiming this. If we can begin to challenge the lazy assumption that the only punitive measure available to the courts is imprisonment we shall have made a little progress.

I am heartened by the examples of best practice in the field of community sentences which have been identified and rewarded by the Howard League for Penal Reform's

Community Programmes Award scheme. Whether in Nottinghamshire, Dorset or Devon and Cornwall, practical schemes which assist offenders to enter (or sometimes re-enter) the world of paid employment can really make a difference and enable them to get back onto the right side of the law.

We must assemble evidence and stories which demonstrate powerfully that even the most persistent of criminals can be turned around by the right intervention at the right time in the right place – in the real world where they are confronted by all the things which made them offend in the first place. And we must keep reminding whoever will listen that jail is definitely not the only punishment that counts. Indeed, for some offenders it will be the worst punishment they could possibly receive.

Kevin Lockyer, NOMS Chief Operating Officer, former Regional Offender Manager, South West

The Value and Importance of Community Sentences and Programmes: the Best Way to Promote Them in Order to Impact on Sentencing

It is a privilege to be asked to contribute to this handbook. I have been a member of the Howard League for Penal Reform for some years. Their support for raising the positive public profile of community sentences has been very welcome. Our campaigning partners are absolutely critical to the future development of work with offenders in the community.

It is ironic that as crime levels have fallen and as the probation service and its partners have increased their knowledge about features of effective work with offenders, public confidence in community sentences has not risen. In fact it has taken several knocks, partly as a result of some high-profile cases, some evidence of poor services and also because of the lack of clearly expressed political confidence. Community sentences have increased by 47% since 1995 but are still not being seen as a satisfactory alternative to imprisonment. More often they are used instead of less serious disposal.

But there are signs that the tide is again turning. Important issues have been accepted by the government from the Corston review of prisons and extensive consultation is taking place on the national Reducing Re-Offending Framework. The NOMS (see glossary) recent move to the Ministry of Justice strengthens the liaison with sentencers and greater public ministerial support has been helpful. The Probation Boards' Association is working closely with senior officials and ministers to ensure that the value of the work of the probation service and its partners is recognised in future commissioning and planning.

Local Probation Area (or Trust) commissioning, much of it undertaken jointly with partners from Drug Action Teams, Supporting People and Local Area Agreements, has the potential to create local community programmes and resources that meet the needs and risks of offenders in different parts of the country.

Community sentences in 2008 provide a powerful mix. They have the capacity to punish, to help, to rehabilitate and to provide oversight where risk of harm is high. They are managed using an internationally validated and comprehensive set of tools and programmes. They are based on the latest research. Consistency of practice has hugely improved since the inception of the NPS for England and Wales in 2001, whose overall performance has increased faster than most other public sector organisations.

Reoffending rates have been reduced significantly and the better we focus the community package on the risk and needs of the offender, the better the results. We should celebrate and publish this success and the Howard League for Penal Reform's Community Programmes Awards are a very good opportunity to do so.

Community sentences are served where the offender lives and can benefit from other local resources, reducing the chances of further offences. They are also able to contribute to the community, most notably through unpaid work. Locally we ask neighbourhoods, who experience high levels of crime, to nominate unpaid work projects through the Community Payback scheme, and this can have a very positive effect on public attitudes to the probation service. Most people, when taken through sentencing exercises on specific cases, make less punitive decisions than the court on the day, and want to find a disposal that stops it happening again. So do most victims.

As a chief officer I am very proud of the range of options that we offer our local courts. The staff think imaginatively about ways in which to communicate the nature of the work under different requirements and sentencers usually say, after a visit, that they are surprised by the complexity of our work. We cannot deliver the work alone and local volunteers and partner agencies are key to the offenders' success. We were delighted that the 'Warbarth' employment partnership project in Cornwall won the Howard League for Penal Reform's Community Programmes Award in 2007. It made a huge difference to the working links and probation staff, as well as boosting the confidence of the offenders and potential employers within the scheme.

Another feature of the best community programmes is their focus on inclusion, particularly for those groups who are marginalised and may experience a very high level of crime. Specific projects have been developed, for example, with migrant workers, refugees and with Muslim community groups, to identify how issues may be resolved, both for victims and for offenders, who are often one and the same.

Finally, I want to return to the interrelationship between community programmes and custody. The Howard League for Penal Reform exists for penal reform. The Carter report (2007) on prisons sets out a programme of reform, not just for the prison service but also proposals for improving the transparency, predictability and consistency of sentencing and the criminal justice system. He proposes a structured sentencing framework and the modification for the use of custody for certain types of low-risk offenders and offences.

If we are to tackle the rising prison population through proposing community sentences as credible alternatives, and naturally I agree that we should, we must also work closely with local partners on tackling low-level nuisance crime and high social need and exclusion. Otherwise the criminal justice system will just absorb more and more people who are there, not necessarily because they are serious criminals, but for other social, economic or health reasons. We will then fill up the prisons with breachers and exacerbate the potentially harmful effects of criminal justice intervention.

In Devon and Cornwall, the Local Criminal Justice Board has been running a project since 2004, which expands the options available to the court for defendants at the lower end of the spectrum. This now forms part of the national community justice programme. Ingredients include a problem-solving approach within the community court, better links between magistrates and specific neighbourhoods to understand the impact of anti-social behaviour, an advice service for defendants and their families at court, and the Community Payback approach to unpaid work described above.

This is a powerful inter-agency project, which harnesses the energies and skills of those public and voluntary sector organisations that are concerned with crime and reoffending reduction. Because it has the capacity to divert low-risk, but needy defendants out of the criminal justice system, it can create headroom, so that community orders can be targeted on those who really need a sustained period of probation work, including many who are currently in prison.

This and all the other community programmes honoured by the Howard League for Penal Reform demonstrate that when we get together we can find powerful solutions. I commend this handbook to you and urge all those connected to the criminal justice system to get out and make those nominations!

Mary Anne McFarlane, Chief Officer, Devon and Cornwall Probation Area (on behalf of the Probation Boards' Association)

Community Programmes Award

Of course we all know the slogans: 'Community sentences cut crime'; 'Community Payback'; 'tough love'; 'prison isn't the answer'; but, to sentencers, these are cumulatively unconvincing. To impress those who sentence, both in the magistrates' court and the Crown Court, the focus has to switch to: 'Why you should trust community sentences'. There is a widespread assumption among sentencers, as in the wider public:

(a) that those sentenced to community sentences regard such an outcome as being 'let off';

(b) that a substantial proportion of those who receive community sentences quickly reoffend;

(c) that where community orders are breached, they are insufficiently rigorously enforced; and

(d) that feeble excuses for non-compliance with community orders are too readily accepted by those responsible for their supervision.

That these urban myths are capable of point-by-point rebuttal is not the issue: the pressing need is to impress on all who pass sentence that community penalties in fact are, and can demonstrably be seen to be, not only a viable alternative to a custodial sentence; but for those for whom they are tailored they are a real improvement on an immediate custodial sentence. They are an improvement because: they address in a practical way the problems, which have caused the offending behaviour, and tackle the causes of those problems:

• properly used and enforced they discourage offenders from repeating their involvement in the criminal justice process;

- they encourage the development of a dialogue between offender and supervisor which is likely to lead to positive improvement in the offender's pro-social functioning;

- where opportunities exist for sentencer supervision, they develop an understanding in both offender and sentencer of the root causes of the offending behaviour and, by addressing those causes, enable the offender to develop self-esteem which tackles those causes; and

- on any view they are cheaper than incarceration.

The community-based schemes outlined in this handbook are paradigms of good practice. As one of the judges of the Howard League for Penal Reform's Community Programmes Award scheme for the past two years it has been a privilege to discover quite how many excellent schemes exist, which have played such a pivotal part in addressing the problems of offenders, and thus effectively tackling reoffending in their areas. My hope is that these exemplars of good practice, which are by no means restricted to the award winners described, may develop their links with local sentencers, so that what they offer can be more widely known in the sentencing community.

Valuable initiatives, such as that of Rethinking Crime and Punishment Phase 2, have brought home to sentencers in the Thames Valley and Cheshire areas the tangible benefits of a dialogue between sentencers, probation officers and offenders, and it is the hope of this contributor that the existence of the Howard League for Penal Reform's initiative will reinforce that message country-wide.

The availability of sentencer supervision and its benefits first came to prominence with the arrival of the drug treatment and testing order in 2000. Many commentators on the reasons for the success of these orders (now the community order with a drug rehabilitation requirement), including both offenders themselves, academics, drug workers and members of the judiciary at all levels with practical experience of the operation of these orders, have identified the availability of continuity of supervision by the initial sentencer as one of the most important (and frankly unexpected) aspects of whether or not such orders will succeed or fail.

Vulnerable defendants frequently only need a framework of support and structure in their lives to avoid reoffending. Such support and structure can be, and frequently is, found in the operation of a community order; but active supervision of a non-custodial penalty by the original sentencer frequently produces positive benefits towards the progress made by offenders, primarily because they have hitherto lacked the experience of an 'authority figure' to take an active interest in their lives.

The lessons which have been learned in relation to those subject to community orders with a drug rehabilitation requirement can be applied equally to other forms of non-custodial sentences. The first example is the new suspended sentence order with a supervision requirement, which will almost certainly include one or more additional requirements of a community order. By virtue of section 191, Criminal Justice Act 2003, such an order may, and ordinarily should, be reviewed periodically by the courts; and the same beneficial consequences follow if the offender is routinely and regularly reviewed by the original sentencer. Such reviews tend to build up support and a relationship between the offender and the sentencer which is as beneficial as that between the offender and an experienced offender manager.

The availability of sentencer supervision can be extended in relation to particular courts or particular areas so as to bring into operation the general supervisory and reviewing role provided by section 178, Criminal Justice Act 2003, which has specifically been brought into effect in relation to the Liverpool Community Justice Centre and the newly launched community justice pilot courts.

It should not require elaboration that if a sentencer can be persuaded to use a non-custodial disposal instead of a short custodial sentence, the availability of sentencer supervision for such offenders may reassure sentencers that compliance with the requirements of the order can be routinely and regularly policed by the sentencers themselves; and may establish a supportive bond between offender and sentencer which challenges and ultimately reduces the pattern of reoffending which currently requires the imposition of a custodial sentence.

His Honour Judge John Samuels QC

The Value and Importance of Community Sentences: How They Can be Strengthened in the Future

The overall aim of any criminal justice system and any sentence imposed by the courts must be to reduce reoffending for the protection of the public. Indeed such principles are enshrined in the Criminal Justice Act 2003, which identified for the first time the five purposes of sentencing as:

- punishment;
- reduction of crime and deterrence;
- reform and rehabilitation;
- protection of the public; and
- reparation.

The focus must not solely be on the offender but also on any victim, either a direct complainant or the public at large. Shoplifting impacts adversely on every member of the public, as does fraud, especially benefit fraud. These are serious crimes and unless the underlying causes of offending are addressed then offending may not be reduced. Courts have a range of sentences available to them – discharges, fines, community orders and custody. In deciding which sentence is appropriate the court will assess:

- the seriousness of the offence as determined by two factors;
- the culpability of the offender;
- what harm the offence actually caused or could cause;
- the impact on victims or the general public; and
- the circumstances of the offender.

These factors determine which purposes of sentencing will be appropriate in each case. Some sentences may meet one purpose, most will meet several. There are claims that punishment must be the prime purpose of sentencing – this may be the case for some offenders. However, sentences have to be effective not only in punishing the offender, but also in ensuring that the underlying reasons for the offending behaviour are addressed. There is no doubt that imprisonment has a place as a sentence, but all too often it serves only to protect the public for a period of time. There are claims that short periods of custody are ineffective in reducing crime and ensuring reform and rehabilitation, supporting the view that community sentences have a more effective impact for the less serious offender. If community sentences are to become more widely used, it is vital that both sentencers and the public have confidence in their effectiveness.

Sentencers are encouraged to examine whether, instead of a custodial sentence, an appropriate community order can be imposed with or without requirements. When used constructively a community sentence can impact significantly on both offenders and the public. If a sentencing court believes that an offender's liberty should be restricted as a form of punishment this can be achieved through a number of requirements: *unpaid work, participation in specified activities, prohibition from certain activities, curfews, residence requirement, supervision, attendance centre for the under 25s.* Others support the principles of reoffending reduction, reform, rehabilitation and reparation through programmes aimed at *changing offending behaviour or treating mental health, drug and alcohol problems.* Such programmes address the causes of crime and show victims that offenders are encouraged and supported to manage their own problems.

However, there are concerns about the impact of community orders. The effectiveness of a court order is often negated by delay. If a Think First programme does not start until five months after imposition it will have no impact and will result in reoffending. The programmes themselves are often too generic. Offenders are only allowed to attend some programmes if they present a risk level which matches the programme's level of intensity and if deemed to have the offending-related needs addressed by the programme. Eligibility and suitability criteria inform which offenders should attend which programmes. This would suggest that criteria are *programme centred instead of offender centred*. Sentencers would have greater confidence in community orders if they were convinced that each programme focused on individual needs through an offender-directed programme.

Many of the Howard League for Penal Reform's Community Programmes Award winners in 2007 did just that. The Nottinghamshire Probation Service Access Team works with unemployed offenders, offering a flexible, creative and realistic approach to remove barriers to employment, training and education. The Dorset Community Service Unit based at Bovington Camp Tank Museum aims to increase the employability of offenders on unpaid work orders (UWOs) and reduce reoffending. Sacro's Another Way Service provides an intense level of support to counter the chaos and mistrust of authority that very frequently characterises the lives of prostitutes. The Sandwell Youth Offending Service supports young persons with a resettlement plan including education, training, basic skills and health issues.

Magistrates welcome such innovative programmes and wish to see them extended more comprehensively across the country. This can be achieved only through greater co-ordination and financial support for such development.

It is also important that the public appreciates that community sentences are not an easy option and immediate action is effective. The Magistrates' Association and the Probation Boards' Association realised the importance of public engagement and five years ago established the Local Crime, Community Sentence joint project. In this project, specially trained sentencers and probation officers engage with the public to help them understand how they deal with crime and offenders. The project involves magistrates and probation officers giving an interactive presentation before answering questions and addressing concerns about how the courts deal with offenders. The format is lively but simple. The audience hears the basic facts about an offence and offender and votes for what it thinks is the right sentence – initially a large proportion chooses the custody option. As more information is revealed about community sentences and their effectiveness, many in the audience change their minds for the same scenario at the end of the session. Collating the evaluations for every presentation over the past five years has clearly demonstrated that once people are given clear and proper information about community sentences they are much less insistent on a custodial sentence.

Magistrates and the public do believe that timely intervention can achieve reform, rehabilitation, reparation and reduction in offending through an adequately funded scheme of offender-focused community-based programmes.

John Thornhill, Deputy Chair,
The Magistrates' Association

CHAPTER 2

Early Interventions With Young People

The Crime and Disorder Act 1998 introduced a greater focus on prevention and early intervention and, in particular, contained measures specifically in the youth justice system to prevent crime and disorder. As a result, providing intervention schemes became an integral part of YOTs.

There were five community programmes recognised by the Howard League for Penal Reform's Award, that focus on factors that heighten the risk of young people offending, for instance factors relating to their personal circumstances, family, social, educational or health, and strengthen 'protective factors', like being in education (Youth Justice Board 2005). These programmes show how there are many complex contributory factors that can lead to a young person offending and the necessity for individually-targeted intervention. Although some of these projects do not work with young people on community sentences, they are providing valuable interventions to support young people in the community.

Rainer's Rapid Action Project (RAP) is an early intervention scheme that offers support for youngsters who are identified as 'at risk' of offending by the police. Outreach youth workers are based in police stations to take referrals. The young people may come into contact with police pre-crime or following their first minor offence. Its effectiveness lies in its early, rapid response and support for young people and their families. It also has the capacity to signpost those most at risk to other specialist services/ agencies.

Y-Pac is an eight-week programme that uses fun interactive exercises, role plays, discussions and artwork to deliver cognitive behavioural activities. Its strengths lie in its blend of skilled practitioners and a programme that enables young people to strive for a better quality of life by using exploration of their past experiences as a springboard.

Leicester, Leicestershire and Rutland Youth Offending Service's (LLRYOS) Short-Term Intervention Programme (STIP) relies on locally recruited volunteers who are trained to deliver one-to-one offending-focused interventions programmes. The same YOS was also recognised by the Howard League for Penal Reform's Community Programmes Award for its Mentoring Project. This project recruits volunteer mentors from all areas of the community and they are involved in reducing crime in their own community through their work with young people. Volunteer involvement also helps to reduce the fear of crime by raising local awareness of the young people's positive work. Both programmes show that positive interventions can help to bring about change in the behaviour of young people at risk of social exclusion and offending, encouraging them to re-engage in education, training and activities in their community. They also show the value of involving local people in changing community perceptions.

Osmaston On-Track, Derby Youth Offending Service's scheme, reduces children's risk of offending and involvement in anti-social behaviour by targeting early interventions at 'known' risk factors. Its ethos is based on the premise that there is no single factor that causes youth crime and that multiple interventions with young people and their families are more likely to be successful.

Rapid Action Project (RAP), Rainer, Essex

Scheme of special merit award 2006

A client's experience

'Louis[1]' was aged 11 years when police gave him a reprimand following a violent incident at school and he was referred to Rainer RAP. He had already been permanently excluded from his junior school. He was verbally and physically disruptive and aggressive towards pupils and teachers. Louis lived with his father and stepmother, as his mother did not want him to live with her.

A RAP worker visited Louis's home and an action plan was put together. The plan tackled his aggression, communication skills, emotional needs, offending behaviour and bullying.

At first Louis was very reluctant to admit responsibility for the behaviour that had got him in trouble with the police. He showed no remorse and had no concept of how his actions affected others. Following intensive intervention, including role play, he began to understand the consequences of the assaults and started to change his behaviour.

Louis made regular visits into the community with his support worker to challenge his negative behaviour towards members of the public and other young people. The RAP worker supported Louis and eventually he gained a place at a weekly boarding school for young people with educational and behavioural needs.

Louis was also helped to improve his relationship with his father and the two of them went on to spend a great deal more time together. As a result Louis has revealed himself to be a bright and confident boy with a real zest for life.

---

1   All names used in case studies and throughout descriptions of community programmes are pseudonyms.

Service provider

Rainer is a registered charity which has been working for over 200 years. It offers under-supported young people a range of services designed to give them the emotional and practical support they need to lead secure and fulfilled lives. Rainer runs around 55 services and projects nationally, working with thousands of young people each year. Many of the young people have been involved with the criminal justice system, are in, or leaving, care, homeless, may be young parents, or are facing serious deficits in their education, affecting their employment prospects. Rainer has been running the Rapid Action Project (RAP) since 2004.

Origins of the programme

Essex Police realised that many children they came across were placing themselves at risk of offending. The police tried to refer them to partner agencies like social care or schools. RAP grew out of the police's frustration with the lack of support for young people and the idea developed for a project with youth workers based in police stations. Essex Police secured the support of the local Children's Fund (see glossary) and Rainer succeeded in winning the tender. In September 2004, Essex Police and Rainer formed a partnership to launch the project as part of the Proactive Essex Police Youth Strategy. It was the first project of its kind in the country but the model has since been replicated in other regions.

Funding

RAP was originally funded through the Children's Fund. This allowed RAP to work with children aged 8 to13 years. Funding has subsequently been secured from the Big Lottery, which changed the target group to those aged 10 to16 years and plans to duplicate the project across the country.

The scheme works in partnership with Essex County Council, Essex Police and Essex Youth Offending Team.

Target group

RAP receives referrals when a young person aged 10 to 16 years:

- receives a police reprimand;
- is engaged in offending behaviour;
- lives in a family where there is a reported incident of domestic violence; or
- is at risk of exclusion from school.

Referrals

Although referrals are mainly made by police officers they can also come from schools or social workers. If a referral is made with the knowledge of the young person and/or family, a RAP worker will phone and make contact straight away and arrange a visit to the young person. If the referral is made without contact with the family or young person, a letter and further information about the service is sent. The scheme aims to make direct contact within two days of a referral.

What does the programme do?

RAP is an early intervention scheme in Essex targeting 10- to 16-year-olds at risk of offending. Participation in the project is voluntary.

Rainer staff are placed in police stations in Harlow, Basildon, Braintree and Rayleigh to provide the low-level, specialist support for children. RAP will receive a referral as soon as a young person comes into contact with the police. This rapid response is the crucial premise on which the project is based. This early intervention to tackle offending behaviour issues aims to prevent the young person from getting sucked into the criminal justice system.

The project aims to:

- provide rapid assistance to young people and their families who become known to the police;
- support young people in crisis, or divert them from offending or anti-social behaviour;
- assist in improving parent's ability to understand, manage and address their children's behaviour and reduce family conflict; and
- work with young people and their families who are referred.

The RAP worker will work with the child and/or family to assess their needs and work out what support RAP is able to provide. RAP believes that forming good relationships with the wider family and doing so quickly improves the chances of providing effective support for the children. Rainer RAP's strategy is to provide flexible direct support on a whole variety of complex issues, but will refer on to other professional agencies if necessary, such as drug support and mental health teams.

The relationship between the RAP worker and the young person is confidential and often takes place away from the home. This allows the young person to 'open up' and makes them feel someone is taking a real interest in them as an individual. RAP workers however will involve the family if appropriate.

Workers develop realistic and measurable action plans with young people. These can cover issues such as anti-social behaviour, anger management, bullying and peer pressure, communication skills, school support, family relationships and community participation through activities and local clubs. They also support young people in the classroom, facilitate meetings with their teachers and help with homework.

RAP usually works with the child over 12 one-hour sessions on a one-to-one basis. These sessions will focus on numerous issues including the consequences of crime, offending behaviour scenarios and the stages of the criminal justice system; or looking at a domestic violence story and discussing how that impacts on the young person. The RAP worker can also act as a mentor. RAP workers can also provide practical support, like ensuring a child attends school. In one instance a truanting schoolgirl was taken to school every morning for four weeks until she felt comfortable and able to go school by herself.

Client visit protocol

RAP staff work on their own with clients unless the police referral suggested that there could be problems with safety. RAP staff would work in pairs if necessary. Many visits take place in school and if the child is not in school, then visits can occur in the family home or in a public place, for example, a café.

RAP staff use a buddy system where, after each visit, they check in with a fellow worker to notify them of their safety.

Client numbers

During its first year of operation, RAP received 422 referrals. Of these, 60% were for young people living with domestic violence.

Monitoring

Staff write a report after each session with the young person. It describes how the session went, how they felt, what the session involved and any issues that need to be dealt with. More detailed reports are made if there needs to be a referral to a support agency.

When work with the child ends, the young person and their family complete a feedback and satisfaction questionnaire. This is used to develop service delivery.

When a case has been closed, the RAP worker will call the young person a few weeks later to make sure everything is OK. They will also call the young person's family approximately one month later to check once again.

Staffing

The project employs five project staff to deliver the face-to-face work with young people and their families. This is the tackling-crime team. The team is line managed by the tackling-crime manager. An administration co-ordinator supports the team. Rainer's Essex area manager is responsible for the project.

The project has a steering group consisting of Rainer staff, police, social services' early interventions service and the YOT (see glossary).

Staff receive training on equality and diversity issues; risk assessment; motivational interviewing; and child protection.

Benefits of the scheme

The rapid response to referrals received means that young people and their families see almost immediate action. They are given an immediate, intense and specialised service tackling problematic issues before the young person and family lose interest in accepting support. Rainer regards the placement of RAP staff within police stations as a way to develop an effective channel of communication between the police, staff and partner agencies.

Evaluation and effectiveness

Statistics from RAP show that only 1% of young people who engaged with the project went on to offend. An internal evaluation of parents'/carers' perceptions showed:

- 70% noted significant improvements in behaviour and anger management in their children;
- 90% noted improvements at school;
- 80% noted significant improvements in self-esteem, self-confidence and self-presentation; and
- 100% noted increased levels of happiness.

Contact details:

Rainer
Shield House
Elizabeth Way
Harlow
Essex CM19 5AR
Tel: 01279 408370

Y-Pac (Young People Affected by Crime and Confidence), Newham Youth Offending Team (NYOT)

Outstanding scheme award 2006

A client's experience

'Jon' came to the attention of the criminal justice system when he was 15 years old. He had committed various offences. He told Y-Pac that he had: ' … locked my mum in the cellar and then held her "man" in a head lock and held the knife close to his face …'.

He had no contact with his father since he was seven years old. At this point he went to live with his grandmother in the Midlands only returning to live with his mother when he was ten years old. His mum had mental heath concerns. She presented all her 'significant male partners' to Jon as 'dad'. Jon was not attending any education provision. He also witnessed domestic violence on an almost daily basis. He had no siblings with whom to share his experiences. Jon had made several suicide attempts. His mother felt she could no longer cope with him.

Jon's Y-Pac referral stated that he had issues with anger, lifestyle concerns and he had used weapons and threatening behaviour to his mother, her partner, other young people and security staff.

Jon started Y-Pac along with six other young people on referral orders. His eight-week programme case diary included the following entries:

Initially Jon was reluctant to engage. Once he realised the workshop did not involve work sheets ('I am not interested in worksheets') and involved interactive exercises followed by discussions, he felt more comfortable. The group created and 'tagged' [signed] a support code (ground rules), which included 'fun in the workshop'. This gave Jon permission to be himself. Jon appreciated the fact that everyone had equal voice and that he was treated with respect and unconditional regard ('you treated me on the level').

From the team building sessions:
Jon excelled in all the activities. He surprised himself as a natural team leader and good team player ('never knew I had it in me!'). Jon was working with Y-Pac when the London tube bombs went off in July 2005. He stated that he did not care if he was blown up. This led Y-Pac staff to suggest his lack of self-value contributed to his offending behaviour.

From the conflict resolution session:
Jon learned new strategies and how he could have dealt with previous situations differently through role play.

From the communication skills session:
In this session Jon saw how body language plays a pivotal role in communication. Jon was extremely articulate in this session significantly adding to the discussion. Y-Pac staff challenge participant's cognitive thinking throughout the programme.

Jon, like all participants, was sent texts after each session to highlight their positive achievements. After the communication skills session, he was sent an affirmation postcard to his home address so he could 'show it off' to others. This is a tool to enable positive communication with significant others.

By week six, Y-Pac should have established trust with the young person. At this point they are asked to disclose their 'autobiography' using an illustrated lifeline. In the lifeline Jon was encouraged to 'talk' about his offending history and provide personal information about his life, family and friends to the group.

When Jon was sharing his lifeline with the group he was symbolically tied up and had a rucksack full of weights on his back. This is meant to represent the baggage and restrictions in their lives and is removed after each significant disclosure is made to the group.

Jon spent the next two weeks using the techniques he learned in his daily life and reporting back to the group on how it had gone. The

Y-Pac programme was encouraging him to let go of his old self and embrace the new future.

Service provider

Y-Pac is a project co-ordinated by Newham Youth Offending Service.

Origins of the programme

The Y-Pac programme was originally developed while its manager worked for Victim Support as a street crime co-ordinator. It was originally designed to support young victims of street crime and sought to reduce their victim-offender cycle. NYOT had used this programme, so the service manager decided to transfer the programme to the YOT (see glossary). Y-Pac resulted and has been running since 2004.

Funding

The Neighbourhood Renewal Fund (see glossary), which gives £32,000, and the Youth Justice Board (YJB) (see glossary), which gives £90,000 via the offender behaviour programmes' budget, funds Y-Pac every year.

Target group

Y-Pac works in partnership with the education, voluntary and statutory sectors, to support young people aged 10 to 17 years who:

- have poor educational attendance levels;
- display challenging behaviour in the home, community or while in education;
- have been predicted to have low educational attainments;
- are identified as at risk of becoming involved in crime and/or anti-social behaviour; or
- are at risk of becoming victims of crime.

What does the programme do?

Y-Pac has a three-tier aim:

- to support young people who are victims of crime and to work to help reduce the victim/offender cycle;
- to prevent young people who are identified as at risk of offending from getting involved in anti-social behaviour, crime and offending; and
- to prevent young people who are subject to reprimands, final warnings or referral orders from reoffending.

Y-Pac works with a diverse range of young people including those who are either loud and are creating a 'whirlwind' of attention around them, or those who are not making noise and are in danger of being forgotten.

Y-Pac believes that experiential training is more effective that conventional classroom training. It uses an eight-week cognitive behavioural activities programme to engage all young people's learning styles using fun interactive exercises, role plays, sculptures, discussions and artwork. The programme encourages young people to identify alternatives to their current motivations, attitude, behaviour, lifestyle and choices. It tries to empower young people to evaluate themselves and take positive steps to address parts of their lives that are not working, either for them or those around them.

The eight-week programme includes:

- learning to become an effective team member;
- understanding, appreciating and working with diversity;
- understanding, minimising and resolving conflict;

- enhancing communication skills, especially becoming aware of how to develop rapport and use body language effectively;
- increasing self-confidence, empathy and self-esteem, with peer acceptance and support; and
- exploring explicit and implicit patterns and how to get individual needs heard and met effectively in a non-violent or aggressive manner.

The programme content is focused on developing the following areas, identified by the child and adolescent mental health service (CAMHS) (see glossary) as resilience factors in children required in achieving non-offending behaviour, including: a positive attitude; problem solving approach; good communication skills; an ability to plan; a capacity to reflect and empathise and think of others.

The NYOT offending behaviour sessions are held on weekday afternoons for an hour and a half after school. Each session has a group of up to 12 young people.

Ten-week programme for young people on a high tariff

Week	Session contents, aims and objectives
1	**Introduction and team building:** Developing rapport, humour, trust and safety within a new group setting; How does the young person behave when meeting new people? What are first impressions and judgements?
2	**Team building and empathy:** Problem solving approach; Thinking behaviour; capacity to reflect; what does empathy mean? Motivation and attitude towards empathising with others.
3	**Difference:** Gangs or groups of friends? What do we know about each other? What are the similarities? How do you react to difference? What are stereotypes?
4	**Conflict:** What causes conflict? The FIDO (see glossary) technique; What are the alternatives other than violent aggressive behaviour? What are the consequences? Ability to form relationships with others.
5	**How are you perceived?** Personal identity; Attitudes towards self and others; Past and current judgements; Building positive attitude and belief towards self; Chosen lifestyle.
6	**Effective communication:** Good communication skills; What does your body language and tone say about you? How do others react to your personal space? What happens when your personal space is violated?
7	**Trust issues:** What does it mean to trust or be trusted? Previous trust issues; How do you trust? Who do you trust? Secure attachment.
8	**Lifelines:** Previous positive and negative experiences; Human baggage; What about forgiveness and breaking free?

Week	Session contents, aims and objectives
9	**The future plan and catalyst for change:** Devising the five-year plan; what are the possible crossroads? What resources and support is available and how would you access them? Capacity to plan; Belief in control rather than fate; Peer pressure; Leadership skills and the strength required.
10	**Moving forward and sourcing a wider support network:** Review of work and the changes experienced through personal observation, group feedback and facilitator feedback; what protective factors can be increased via the use of other agencies eg YISP; endings including letter to self to be sent in 6 months time

All young people attending the NYOT offender behaviour programme sign a contract in which they agree to attend and participate on the scheme, as well as the standard of their behaviour whilst on the programme.

Young people are sent a text or called on the day prior to each session as a reminder. It also provides the young people with an opportunity to explain if they cannot attend that session.

The last session is used to congratulate young people, with each one receiving a certificate of attendance and completion of the course.

Client numbers

Between April 2004 and September 2007, Y-Pac has worked with:

- 306 young people subject to a reprimand, warning or referral order (see glossary);
- 26 young people identified as 'at risk' of offending; and
- 40 young people who have been victims of crime.

Staffing

The project has four full-time staff:

- an interventions co-ordinator who develops and delivers the programmes;
- a Y-Pac facilitator who delivers the programmes in schools;
- a Y-Pac offender behaviour programme worker based at NYOT; and
- an offender behaviour facilitator, who delivers the programme specifically on robbery and burglary.

Five volunteers also work with Y-Pac.

Volunteers

The volunteers are recruited through NYOT and used across a range of its programmes. All volunteers will complete the YJB foundation training which covers a range of issues including child and adolescent development; young people and crime; risk and protective factors linked to crime; effective communication; and the youth justice system.

The potential Y-Pac volunteer is also required to complete a season of shadowing with an experienced practitioner.

Once working with Y-Pac, volunteers are subject to quality assurance audits. This means that the Y-Pac co-ordinator will make an unannounced visit to where the volunteer is working. Volunteers co-facilitate the sessions. The visit is to ensure that the programme is delivered effectively.

Monitoring and evaluation

All young people complete review questionnaires to assess their offending behaviour at the beginning and end of the programme. This is by a service user review, midway through, and at the end of, the programme.

The young people complete feedback sheets after each session to evaluate how they felt during the session, what they learnt and what they enjoyed. This becomes their Y-Pac diary. The information is collated on the YOT (see glossary) data system and on individual case files for future reference.

Each week young people are asked:

- to rate how safe they felt to talk about and share their experiences in the group on a scale of 1 to 10;
- one learning point they took away from the session and explain it;
- what they would like to have seen done differently and why; and
- what they enjoyed about the session and why.

The very last session of each programme is used for the young people to evaluate the impact of the programme as a whole in terms of confidence, awareness of their actions, and self-esteem. Young people are also asked to rate and provide feedback on the workshop leaders.

Example of service user feedback form

Name of young person	Date of birth	Offence	Order	Case-worker	Interview date
"John"					

Feedback form completed by caseworker/~~careers officer/ education officer/ other~~ (delete as appropriate)

How did the young person rate the project?

-3	-2	-1	0	1	2	3
very negative	negative	some negative indication	neutral	some positive indication	positive	very positive

If scored below 0 what would have scored the project higher?

Said that he really enjoyed the workshop and found it to be a positive experience

What did the young person get from the project?

Group problem solving sessions useful and in particular one to one sessions with caseworker re truanting. Has turned around and John feels refocused at school.

What did you learn about yourself as a result of the project?

That I was easily led and had a short temper. John was proud when he received his YPAC certificate.

What did you learn about other people and how are you towards them?

That some people appeared happy on the outside when sad on the inside. John felt that he got on well with everyone and that they were nice to him.

How will you use the learning taken from the project and use it in real life?

Not to trust people on first meeting and not to jump into situations. To use better judgement.

What changes have your parent(s)/carers noticed about you since completing the project?

That I am more focussed at school, more confident and conscientious.

Y-Pac data provide information about the outcomes of all the young people it has worked with since it started in 2004:

- of the 306 young people working with Y-Pac following a reprimand, warning or referral order, 76% had not reoffended (compared with a 31% reconviction rate across NYOT);
- of the 26 people identified at risk of offending, 88% had not entered the criminal justice system;

and

- of the 40 victims of crime Y-Pac had worked with, 97% had not entered the criminal justice system.

The effectiveness of Y-Pac has been linked to the blend of skilled practitioners with a programme that helps young people to explore past experiences as a tool to enable them to develop new strategies to strive for a better quality of life.

Contact details:

Shelly Khaled
Training & Development Manager
Newham Youth Offending Team
192 Cumberland Road
Plaistow
London
E13 8LT

Tel: 0208 430 2361

Email: shelly.khaled@newham.gov.uk

Short-Term Interventions Project (STIP), Leicester, Leicestershire and Rutland Youth Offending Service (LLRYOS)

Outstanding scheme award 2005

A client's experience

'Sarah' was 14 years old when she received a final warning. She admitted assaulting a fellow pupil at school. A volunteer mentor worked with her for six sessions to address victim awareness issues, consequences and implications of further offending and anger management.

Sarah had recently moved to live with her father following arguments with her mother. A volunteer visited her mother before starting to work with Sarah. This led to a range of agencies being identified to provide extra support for Sarah's parents and siblings.

Sarah's mentor helped her to identify the causes of her anger and to develop less aggressive ways of dealing with situations. Her behaviour improved immensely as a result of working with her mentor. She disclosed to her volunteer mentor that she worried about her health but would not go to a doctor as she was frightened of both the doctor and of any possible diagnosis. The volunteer encouraged this young person. Eventually Sarah sought medical advice.

A volunteer's experience

When I moved to England from America, I decided that my career in marketing and sales wasn't fulfilling. I decided there was no better way to give a part of yourself and feel you are doing something good for society than to volunteer. I have now been volunteering with the interventions team for over a year and a half.

I learnt about the team through a YOT reparation worker I called, and set up an interview to discuss the project. I was made to feel very welcome and they guided me through the process of helping young people who have been offered this 'last chance'. Once I had been accepted as a mentor

I had induction training and topped it up regularly with additional information and training.

The great thing about this team was that they were flexible. You can choose when you take on a new case and the amount you can handle. They tried to give you an area that was close to you so that travelling didn't become an issue.

The main objective of the project was to help young people make decisions, young people who needed your guidance on where to find different outlets for their future. Many of the young people were grateful for my input and were very appreciative. Young people sometimes needed people from outside of their environment to give a different perspective on their life. I've met many lovely young people who have not gone back into offending due to the interventions team.

Service provider

The interventions team is administered by LLRYOS. It is supported by Leicestershire Constabulary, Leicestershire and Rutland Probation Area, Leicester City Council, Leicestershire County Council and Rutland County Council. The short-term interventions project is one of many programmes run by the LYOS early interventions team.

Origins of the programme and funding

The project started in 1987 and was funded by Leicestershire Police. It was known as the Leicestershire Young Offenders' Diversion Scheme. The Crime and Disorder Act 1998 (see glossary) meant that the project moved into the YOS's jurisdiction and it was renamed. Leicester City YOT (see glossary) and Leicestershire YOS jointly fund the project.

Target group

The STIP is a multi-agency project targeting young people aged 10 to 17 years who have been given a final warning (see glossary).

Referrals

LLRYOS is notified of young people prior to the police issuing a final warning to enable them to carry out an assessment. During this time the young person is bailed. The YOS officer, who is often a seconded police officer, will refer the young person to the interventions team.

The LLRYOS then carry out an Asset assessment (see glossary) on the young person to identify the factors likely to increase their risk of reconviction, and therefore measure the level of intervention required and tackle issues where they can provide support. An Asset score of between 6 and 15 means there is a low to medium risk of the young person being reconvicted and therefore will result in a referral to the STIP. A score higher than this can result in a referral to the Mentoring Project – see page 68 – where longer and more intense levels of interventions are deemed necessary. However, there are occasions when a higher score is referred to the STIP, depending upon the young person's circumstances.

All young people referred to the STIP come to the interventions team with a bail date. Before this date a volunteer will need to be matched and allocated to that young person, so that work can start as soon as the final warning is given. The young person is sent a letter to notify them that a volunteer will start working with them.

Once a referral is made, the STIP manager and their mentor will visit the young person, usually at home, to encourage them to engage with the project. Volunteer mentors are allocated one young person at a time. However, the number of allocations may increase with confidence and experience to a maximum of three cases at a time.

What does the programme do?

The objectives of the project are to:

- maintain and develop a task force of volunteers to deliver effective intervention with young people;
- make sure that young people are dealt with swiftly, fairly and appropriately;
- assist young people who have offended to understand the full implication of their actions, for themselves and others;
- provide constructive intervention, which reduces the risk of reoffending by young people;
- encourage young people to make amends for their actions by considering the needs of victims and the community;
- help young people to develop a sense of personal responsibility and to encourage them to become confident members of the community; and
- involve parents where appropriate.

STIP is based on a voluntary, one-to-one relationship between a young person and a supportive adult. Parents of all young people are asked to sign a consent form allowing the intervention to take place.

Volunteers provide support, guidance and advice to counter the influence of inappropriate peer pressure, and help young people change their attitudes and behaviour, develop social and personal skills, and overcome difficulties. The STIP believes that volunteers have an important role in steering disadvantaged and disaffected young people away from crime and anti-social behaviour. They provide positive role models and a way of giving them practical support, for instance helping young people return to education, training and employment. The volunteer may also facilitate ongoing support from other agencies, although the actual referral has to be made by LLRYOS.

For each case, a contract is signed by all parties. This enables the volunteer and young person to write an action plan and use their subsequent sessions effectively. The contract will address all the issues identified in the Asset form.

Volunteers will work with a young person for six to eight weeks. The volunteer and young person will meet weekly. They can meet at the young person's house or out in the community, for example, in a café, library or community centre. The volunteer will assist, support and motivate the young person in developing skills and appropriate attitudes which will assist them in achieving and sustaining their personal goals. The volunteer may also refer the young person to other agencies within the community to encourage them to access ongoing support. All referrals to other agencies/projects are made by the LLRYOS caseholder following identification and discussion of further needs with the volunteer and interventions manager. The volunteer and young person's area of work can include tackling anger management, peer pressure, looking at the victims and the consequences of their actions. All volunteers on the scheme have access to resources, including videos, games, worksheets etc. from the LLRYOS library, to use when working with young people.

Example of worksheet used to help young people understand the consequences of their actions

What if?	
Aim:	To explore with the young person general consequences of burglary (not necessarily their offence); To build up trust; and To get them thinking, without feeling intrusive about their own offence. Subsequent activities will explore more specifically their own offence.
Method:	Using Jenga and discussion.
Resources:	Jenga, pens, adhesive putty and scissors.

Both the young person and the volunteer working with them should write out potential consequences of burglary considering the following areas: the offender; family and friends; the victim; and, the police.

Write out the consequences, one per square, using either a word or picture that you will understand. You do not need to write sentences. Fill in as many squares as possible.

Then cut and stick the squares onto a side of the Jenga blocks (one per block). Then set up the game, making sure the sides with the paper are facing outwards, and that they are placed evenly around the tower.

Once this is completed, play the game as normal, but pull out your consequences and then explain why you have put them down, explore any issues or ask further questions as the game progresses.

continued on page 64

When the tower falls, talk through any consequences that have note been discussed. Also make the connection between the game and consequences: that when people offend it can ruin their and other people's lives, it can be like the tower, lives are ruined and it can take ages to build them up again.

At the end of the process the young person will receive a certificate to acknowledge their work with the STIP.

Client contact protocol

Volunteers are required to check in and notify staff of their safety after each session with a young person. Volunteers are also matched with a buddy – a fellow volunteer. They will check in with their buddy as well.

Volunteers are not allowed to give any personal details, for example, their last name or contact numbers, to young people.

Client numbers

For the year ending November 2007, STIP received 274 referrals. It carries a caseload of 250.

Monitoring

Volunteers are required to complete weekly contact sheets for the STIP team. Project staff will also directly contact volunteers to discuss cases. All information is compiled on the LLRYOS computer system for future monitoring.

Staffing

The interventions manager in LLRYOS oversees the project. The STIP consists of one full-time manager and one part-time administrative support worker. The project has 85 volunteers working with the young people.

Volunteers

Volunteers from all areas of the community are recruited to work with the young people on the scheme. Leicestershire covers a large geographical area, which incorporates large inner-city estates, and rural areas. It has a diverse ethnic mix and STIP aims to reflect this diversity. Volunteers receive only travel expenses.

Volunteers are recruited using information leaflets that are circulated within the community and through presentations made at volunteer centres, leisure centres and community centres. The project also advertises and promotes itself in the local media.

Volunteers complete a formal application, which is supported by two satisfactory references. Potential volunteers will then be asked to participate in an informal interview. All volunteers are Criminal Records Bureau (CRB) (see glossary) checked. However, people with criminal convictions can be recruited if the offence took place at least six months previously. Searches are made of the Child Protection Register (see glossary).

Once recruited, volunteers undergo the one-day YJB (see glossary) foundation programme training. It provides core learning for all volunteers and covers the issues that are central to understanding and working with young people who have offended or who are at risk of doing so. Topics covered include child development, how their own values, beliefs and preconceptions can influence their attitude and responses towards young people who offend, their families, and the victims of crime.

In addition, volunteers receive specific training about the project. This is delivered over two compulsory evening sessions. This training takes place each quarter with approximately 15 participants. The first session gives information on the project, its processes and policies and what is expected from a volunteer. The second session looks at specific issues like drugs awareness and safeguarding and child protection policies.

In addition, there are usually 10 to 12 sessions throughout the year with external agencies to support volunteers' initial training. In the past this has included probation staff providing training on domestic violence and looking at the impact on young people; anger management; and sexual heath training.

Volunteers receive ongoing support from a specific STIP team member, who could be an experienced volunteer, the interventions manager or an interventions worker.

Volunteers also receive an annual appraisal.

Evaluation and effectiveness

STIP figures show that 85% of young people who take part on the scheme do not reoffend. STIP constantly reviews its effectiveness through client feedback. When a young person leaves the project, they and their family are asked to complete an evaluation. Volunteers are also asked to provide feedback.

Contact details:

Debbie Stobbs
Project Manager
Short-Term Interventions Project
Interventions Team, Leicester
Leicestershire and Rutland Youth Offending Service
Suite 4, Bridge Park Plaza
Bridge Park Road
Thurmaston
Leicester
LE4 8BL

Tel: 0116 2606000

Email: DStobbs@leics.gov.uk

Interventions Team Mentoring Project, Leicester, Leicestershire and Rutland Youth Offending Service (LLRYOS)

Outstanding scheme award 2005

A client's experience

'Shawn' was 16 years old when he was referred to the project. A meeting was set up with him and his family at home. At the initial meeting with his mentor, Shawn and his mother explained that the situation at home was very difficult due to his behaviour. He refused to go to school, mixed with a peer group involved in reckless activity and used drugs. His parents were considering evicting him from home.

Shawn had a final warning and was assessed by the police as being at risk of further offending. During the next nine months, the mentor worked with him to address peer pressure, victim awareness, consequences and implications of further offending, anger management, drug awareness, leisure, employment and training.

At the six-month review meeting, Shawn and his father were present. Shawn reported that he felt confident to challenge his friends and walk away when they were involved in activities that could result in an offence being committed. Shawn had control over his anger, he was not using any drugs, and had applied to go to college. His father reported seeing a positive change in him, he was more motivated, abided by house rules and the atmosphere at home was calm and pleasant. His father stated that the mentor had supported Shawn and been a positive influence. He felt that they could build on the progress that had been made.

Shawn was offered an apprenticeship and hoped to gain a college place; he was positive about his future.

Service provider

The interventions team is managed by LLRYOS. It is made up of the Leicestershire Police Service, Leicestershire and Rutland Probation Area, Leicester City Council, Leicestershire County Council and Rutland County Council.

Origins of the programme and funding

The YJB (see glossary) initially funded the programme for 12 months in 2000. Its success led to Leicester City YOT (see glossary) and Leicestershire YOS providing permanent funding. The project estimates that it spends £7 on volunteers' travel and subsistence per case per month.

The team is also supported by YOS prevention services, which allows the use of their resources.

Target group

The mentoring project is a multi-agency project targeting young people aged 10 to 17 years at the final warning (see glossary) stage and young people on court orders like referral orders.

Referrals

When a young person is issued with a final warning the police will then notify LLRYOS. This will trigger an Asset (see glossary) assessment. If the assessment gives an Asset score of 15 or more a referral is made to the interventions team.

A young person will be sent a letter notifying them of their referral and the allocation of a mentor. The mentoring project manager and the volunteer mentor will then visit the young person to encourage them to engage with the project. This meeting will generally take place at the young person's home.

Mentors are allocated one young person at a time to work with; however, exceptionally, volunteers have a caseload of two or three young people. Volunteers' travel expenses are reimbursed.

What does the programme do?

The project uses restorative justice principles to help young people come to terms with, and make amends for, their offence and then move forward with their life. It is a voluntary, one-to-one relationship between a young person and a supportive adult.

By providing support, guidance and advice, mentors aim to:

- counter the influence of inappropriate peer pressure;
- help young people change their attitudes and behaviour for the better;
- develop social and personal skills; and
- overcome difficulties.

Mentors will be asked to work with a young person for a minimum of three months to a maximum of a year. Young people and mentors are carefully matched. This relationship is pivotal to the success of the process. The key attributes used to match mentors and young people are gender, ethnicity, geographical location, skills, attributes, knowledge and experience. Mentors provide positive role models and practical support to young people involved in the youth justice system. They also help young people access or return to education, training and employment, as well as encourage them to pursue leisure activities.

At the first visit, the young person and their mentor will agree the basis of an action plan. The young person's family will also get a copy of the signed agreement and they will be asked to sign a consent form. LLRYOS believes that a structured approach using action plans that specify a time period, have achievable outcomes and measure progress, helps to keep the focus and boundaries of the mentoring relationship. The young person is able to see progress and build on that success.

A young person will meet and work with their mentor weekly on a one-to-one basis for an hour. The mentor will assist, support and motivate the young person in areas of agreed work. This may include tackling anger management, peer pressure, looking at the victims of crime and the consequences of their actions.

If the young person does not comply with the action plan, for instance by not attending a planned meeting with a mentor, another is arranged. If, again, at the second meeting the young person is absent, a letter will be sent to the family informing them of the situation and enquiring whether the young person still wants to work with the mentor. Finally, project staff will visit the young person and family to discuss reasons for non-compliance, looking at whether the mentor has been an appropriate match, and whether the activities or interventions can be changed to engage the young person on the programme.

Every three months there is a case review meeting. If targets remain unmet, then further action plans and goals are put into place and the work continues. Should all the targets have been met, a final meeting is set up with the mentor, mentoring manager, young person and their family to talk about progress and future plans.

Client visit protocol

All mentors check in and notify LLRYOS staff of their safety after each session with a young person. Mentors are matched with a buddy – a fellow mentor – with whom they also check in after each session. Mentors are not allowed to give any personal details, for example, their last name or contact numbers, to young people.

Client numbers

For the year ending October 2007, 142 referrals were accepted.

Monitoring

Mentors are required to complete monthly contact sheets for LLRYOS documenting the young person's progress. Project staff also maintain telephone contact with mentors. All this information is compiled on the LLRYOS computer system for future monitoring. Information from case review meetings is also added.

Mentors receive a supervision session every three months. This helps to maintain the professional relationship between the mentor and client. Mentors are supported as they plan towards the end of the relationship.

Staffing

The interventions manager in LLRYOS oversees the project. The mentoring project has two full-time staff members: a mentoring manager and a mentoring worker. Clerical support is provided by the YOS. The project has 90 volunteer mentors working with the young people.

Volunteers

See page 65, for information about the recruitment and training of volunteers.

Evaluation and effectiveness

The mentoring project statistics showed that 80% of young people who took part on the scheme did not reoffend once they had completed it.

The mentoring project is under constant review to examine its effectiveness. During each mentoring relationship, reviews are undertaken every three months. Young people, their carers, mentors and the police all provide feedback on the process.

Contact details:

Jane Mooney
Mentoring Manager
Interventions Team, Leicester
Leicestershire and Rutland Youth Offending Service
Suite 4, Bridge Park Plaza
Bridge Park Road
Thurmaston
Leicester
LE4 8BL

Tel: 0116 2606000

Email: JEMooney@leics.gov.uk

Osmaston On-Track, Derby Youth Offending Service

Outstanding scheme award 2006

A client's experience

The Smith family started to work with the project after the boys attended a summer youth club in Osmaston park. The three boys were 'Shawn' aged 8 years, 'David' aged 10 years and 'Liam' aged 12 years. The family were from a travelling background. It was clear they were a close-knit family who looked out for each other. While on the summer club, the boys would openly plan to gang up on other young people.

All three boys were excluded from school and were well known locally for causing trouble, breaking windows, possessing offensive weapons and stealing bikes. They were often involved in fights. The oldest of the brothers, Liam, had been on a YOS anti-social behaviour contract for stealing a car.

After Liam was excluded from school, he started attending the project's exclusion class where he did his schoolwork and took part in wider education classes on issues like drug misuse. However, there were problems. Liam would warm up the end of a biro and attempt to burn people with it, including the project staff. He succeeded in burning the stomach of a staff member.

On-Track staff responded by persuading Mrs Smith to allow all of her sons to attend a fire safety class. This took one hour per week and it was completed in their own time. Eventually they all behaved on the course and enjoyed it.

Since attending On-Track the boys are better behaved and more aware of the consequences of their actions. Two of the boys have been coming home regularly from school with merits. One of them has received a certificate from On-Track for his outstanding accomplishments and contributions. The boys will now walk away from trouble rather than starting it, or actually step in and prevent incidents from happening.

Service provider

Osmaston On-Track is managed and delivered by Derby Youth Offending Service (DYOS).

Origins of the programme and funding

On-Track is an early intervention and prevention programme that was established following the Home Office Crime Reduction Programme in 1999. It was selected as one of the 24 deprived and high-crime areas to develop community-based pilot projects to target children who were 'at risk' of becoming future offenders. The DYOS won three years' funding from the Children's Fund (see glossary) in Derby, and the project was launched in 2002.

It aims to reduce potential crime amongst 5- to 13-year-olds in the Osmaston and Allenton areas of Derby, by targeting the 35 most 'at risk' young people and providing them with a positive role model. The project is based in, and works for, the community, with line management provided by the preventions manager at the DYOS.

Target group

Local agencies, such as the police, social services, housing, schools and local community refer 'at risk' young people to the project; however children only attend the project on a voluntary basis. The children are drawn from the Osmaston and Allenton areas of Derby. They are aged 5 to 13 years. The project targets the 35 children deemed to be the most 'at risk'.

Referrals

Project staff meet with other local agencies to explain their work. They will also send them information and invite referrals. They particularly target schools in the catchment area for referrals at the end of the academic year.

When the project receives a referral for a child and they feel that the project can support them they will visit the young person at home. This visit is often unannounced. During the visit staff will talk with the family and child about the project. If the family agrees to the type of interventions offered, the young person is assessed using the DYOS Onset assessment tool (see glossary). Following assessment every child is allocated a mentor who is matched as far as possible to the young person, taking into account similar interests, ethnicity, gender etc. This mentor should stay with the child during their time with the project.

What does the programme do?

The aim of the project is to reduce offending levels of young people aged between 5 and 13 years and ensure that fewer people are victims of crime by:

- promoting attendance and attainment in school as well as providing alternative education to children not in school;
- reducing bullying and racial incidents committed by 5- to 13-year-olds; and
- promoting healthy living and encouraging physical sustainable activities.

On-Track has a team of young project workers with a good knowledge of the area, who also work as mentors. They work individually with the children and encourage them to take part in a constructive and positive activity each week. Initially many children are hard to engage on the programme, so mentors offer a capture activity to hook them, like a visit to a snooker hall. Once a positive relationship has been built, more sustainable activities are encouraged such as arts, dance or drama. The project is a multi-agency partnership, which helps sustain activities for the children. All activities are presented as fun and provide new experiences. Many of the activities are designed to be stimulating and engaging, whilst also having some developmental or social learning function, such as improving social skills.

The project also uses one-to-one activities with project mentors to encourage children to think about the consequences of crime and explain how their actions affect other people in the community. Mentors have devised a 'consequences awareness' worksheet to aid their victim awareness work. Other sessions focus on improving children's overall academic performance or their general health.

The project engages children in diversionary activities like after school or school holiday clubs that give them something to do while under adult supervision.

Project activities include:

- Exclusion club – providing children with help completing school work, with regular trips to the library and museums to support classroom learning;
- Bike project – working with Derbyshire Police. The police provide old bikes for the children to repair which are then given to young people in the community who do not have a bike or it has been stolen;
- Graffiti workshops;
- Internet café visits; and
- Allenton primary behaviour improvement programme project – provides classroom support to children in their lessons.

Example of two week programme for young people

Monday	Tuesday	Wednesday	Thursday	Friday	Saturday
Bank holiday	11—1pm Outreach 1—3pm Basketball Or 1—4 pm Music technology (4 people)	11—1pm Outreach 1-3pm Football Or 1—4pm Photography project (8 people) 4.30—7pm Megazone	11—1pm Outreach 1—4pm Dance workshop (10 people) Or 1-2.30pm Horse riding (8 people) 4—7pm Cinema trip	11—4pm Trip to American Adventure (12 people)	2.20pm Football (7 people)

Monday	Tuesday	Wednesday	Thursday	Friday	Saturday
11—1pm Outreach 1—4pm Animation project (12 people)	11—1pm Outreach 1—3pm Football Or 1—4 pm Music technology (5 people)	11—1pm Outreach 1—4pm Animation project (4 people) 2—3.30pm Horse riding (8 people)	12 noon Go to Edale (21 young people and 4 staff)		Return from Edale at 3pm

The project will work with young people until they reach the age of 13 years. Support will stop only if the child moves from the area or they no longer require any support.

Client numbers in the last year

The project targets 35 'at risk' young people. Each targeted young person receives at least five hours of interventions each week. During 2007, the project worked with 39 'at risk' children.

Monitoring and evaluation

The Children's Fund set the project targets based on the number of young people attending various activities offered by the project, including:

- Be Healthy – football, swimming, dance, soft play, boxing;
- Stay Safe – fire safety classes, anti-bullying lunch club;
- Enjoy and Achieve – Riley's Snooker Hall, Internet Café, Playhouse, Cinema, Q-Arts, bowling;
- Make a Positive Contribution – bike project, music sessions at Stone Soup, graffiti workshops; and
- Achieve Economic Wellbeing – park visits, library, museum, exclusion class, homework clubs.

Together the mentor and child will write a report about each session highlighting the type of activity, the number of hours and the child's behaviour during the session. This is recorded on the DYOS UMIS (see glossary) database system. Should a child not comply with the rules they are excluded from fun sessions until project staff assess that their behaviour has improved.

At the end of the contact period children complete an exit questionnaire. It focuses on the child's behaviour, which aspects they enjoyed and what they thought of the programme. This information is sent to the DYOS and it is used to evaluate the project.

Children are involved in the planning and evaluation of the project through formal and informal consultations. They are very clear about what they want to get involved in and how they feel the project is working for them. One young person wrote to the project to tell them what difference it had made to them:

I met On-Track when they posted a leaflet through my door. I have been to Cromford, American Adventure and Laser Quest and the youth club. I have been practising my reading with Nigel. I have made new friends. My mum and Nigel are proud of me and I made a CD. Thank you On-Track for taking me on trips. I like Nigel and Laina. I can't wait to go horse riding and like school now.

Staffing

The project employs a full-time co-ordinator and two part-time youth workers/mentors. The assistant head of DYOS line manages the project.

Every six weeks staff receive supervision sessions. The project office is in the community, but staff visit the DYOS on a weekly basis for staff meetings.

Benefits of the scheme

The project has built up excellent relationships in the community, especially with parents. Parents, in particular, were initially wary of the project, fearing professional intervention in their family life. The impact of the project can be found in this extract from a letter from a parent:

Just a note to say thank you for all the support and help you have given to me and Tony. Tony has turned himself around this past year and he has a lot more respect for adults and other peers. He has taken well to Laina and to other females and I feel it is down to On-Track. He bonds really well with Nigel and I was surprised he enjoyed it at Edale. The report I was given back made me so proud of him. I think On-Track had been a great part in turning Tony's attitude around. I only hope he carries on going forward and not backwards. He has achieved so much; thank you all so much.

This project has been successful in changing perceptions in the local community and helping to reduce the fear of crime. One example is the local youth group On-Track established in a local church. The young people felt they had some ownership of the church and it was no longer vandalised. Project staff still attend many community group meetings to hear local concerns and talk about the project.

Contact details:

Laina Richardson
Osmaston On-Track, Project Co-ordinator
40 Addison Road
Allenton
Derby
DE22 1AQ

Tel: 07799 076171

Email: laina.richardson@btconnect.com

CHAPTER 3

Community Programmes Dealing With Factors That Contribute to Offending

Community sentences can be a very effective way of dealing with those factors that can contribute to people committing crimes like an excessive use of alcohol. In the first three years of the Howard League for Penal Reform's Community Programmes Award, Sacro, the Scottish community justice organisation, has secured three awards. All three community programmes focus on helping people deal with the factors: problematic alcohol use; drug use among street sex workers; and working with people who are perpetrators of domestic violence. Sacro's aim is to reduce conflict and offending and make communities safer. Its work has shown that a community sentence that has a treatment requirement, particularly if it is a tailored treatment programme, can be extremely effective in reducing offending behaviour. All three of Sacro's programmes offer sentencers community options that actually provide support while addressing offending behaviour.

The Howard League for Penal Reform's own research (The Howard League for Penal Reform 2006) showed that much emphasis is placed on providing drug-related programmes, yet when asking young men what directly influenced their offending behaviour, alcohol was often a more prominent factor. Sacro's alcohol programme demonstrates the importance of providing an appropriate, effective and well-used programme for addressing alcohol-related offending in the community. It enhances an existing probation sentence and enables people to be critical of their own behaviour and challenge each other in a safe group context. This service encourages positive personal change that, in turn, it is hoped, will help ensure community safety.

Sacro's work plays an important role in Edinburgh's overall strategy to reduce harm and provide street sex workers with possible exit strategies. The evidence produced by Sacro's Another Way Service shows its success in helping women stop street sex working by supporting them to reduce or stop their drug use and its knock-on effect to reduce offending behaviour. This service provides street sex workers with information and advice about treatment services, harm reduction measures and a wide variety of relevant health, housing, employment and social services for women (but it can also be provided for men). Sacro's work is unique and extremely successful in its ability to engage with this difficult-to-reach group.

Sacro's third award was in recognition of its work with domestic abuse perpetrators and their victims. Sacro's Domestic Abuse Group is part of a community-based intervention system to reduce the risk of men being violent and abusive to women and children. Its strength lies in providing a structured environment where service users can explore their behaviour and the impact of this on themselves and others. The work focuses on encouraging positive, achievable change.

Alcohol Education Probation Service (AEPS), Sacro, Edinburgh

Outstanding scheme award 2006

A client's experience

'Allan' had a long history of offending whilst under the influence of alcohol. He felt that he could not stop drinking, as it was a habit. He lived with his partner who was also a problematic drinker. Sacro assessed Allan as suitable for AEPS after he had received an 18-month probation order. It was a condition of the order. Eight weeks after his sentence 'Allan' started the programme. Allan displayed a willingness to address his alcohol use and was constantly enthusiastic to apply the material learned at AEPS to his daily life.

Before starting the programme Allan knew nothing about the impact of alcohol. After the first two sessions it was clear he had begun to develop an understanding about what alcohol is and how it affects the body. This was particularly important for Allan, as he had been identified as having a number of health issues resulting from alcohol but he had not understood the implications for him.

Allan recognised that he made a lot of excuses for his behaviour. As he progressed through the programme he realised the impact that alcohol could have on this behaviour and how he often flew off the handle when he consumed alcohol. He saw that he used alcohol to express his anger. He also admitted that it was his feelings prior to getting drunk and not the alcohol that made him act the way he did. He described incidents to the group and eventually was able to disclose to them his strategies for walking away and cooling off.

Allan has now reduced his alcohol consumption. He has achieved this, in part, by focusing on his son whom he had not seen in a long time prior to attending AEPS. He also used other strategies to control his drinking including pacing himself and swapping some alcoholic drinks for soft ones.

Allan completed the group over six months ago. He has not reoffended. He describes a happy and pleasant lifestyle with a considerable reduction in drinking. He is now looking for new accommodation and seeking regular contact with his son.

Service provider

Sacro is an independent charity which aims to promote community safety across Scotland through providing high-quality services to reduce conflict and offending. Sacro is committed to developing new and innovative ways of working and influencing the development of government policies and of legislation. It provides services in conflict resolution, criminal justice and youth justice, based on the values of mutual respect, recognising and valuing diversity, personal responsibility, society's responsibility to all its members, capacity for change and to work together to reduce conflict and repair harm.

Origins of the programme and funding

Since 1991, Sacro has provided group work programmes for people who relate their use of alcohol to their offending.

The City of Edinburgh and Midlothian Council fund AEPS (£50,000 from Edinburgh and £10,000 from Midlothian Council). This grant has been static for the last five years so additional funding is being sought.

Target group and client assessment

AEPS takes referrals from men and women who acknowledge that their offending is alcohol related. Clients acknowledge that their offending could be reduced if their alcohol use, particularly in specific situations, was under control.

Clients have to be:

- aged 16 years and over;
- living in, or are returning to, Edinburgh and Midlothian area;
- motivated to attend the service;
- being considered for, or subject to, a probation order; and
- acknowledge their offending behaviour is alcohol related.

Social workers make referrals to the programme by contacting AEPS staff. Where potential clients meet the criteria they will be asked to attend an assessment interview. Prior to this interview, background information will be sought such as the client's current offence, a social enquiry report, the procurator fiscal's (see glossary) list of previous convictions, and any risk assessments that have been undertaken. The interview itself will last about an hour and a half, at the end of which a decision will be made as to whether or not the client is suitable for the programme. The assessment process will:

- clarify the person's pattern of alcohol use (and/or drug use if appropriate);
- explore how the pattern emerged;
- identify links with offending behaviour;
- explore motivation to change; and
- identify resources and actions that could facilitate a change in behaviour.

Planning meetings will take place prior to starting a programme. These meetings involve the client, Sacro staff and the supervising social worker. The meetings are used to discuss expectations, purpose of attendance and a service agreement to be signed by all parties.

What does the programme do?

The rationale for the project is that much offending is linked to alcohol misuse. It is unique as it tackles alcohol issues from the perspective of offending behaviour. It specifically uses group work methods with the aim of helping individuals to develop and adopt more positive and law-abiding lifestyles. The programme aims to enable people to:

- increase their knowledge and understanding of alcohol and its effect;
- examine their own use of alcohol and assess its effects on their offending behaviour;
- acquire skills and confidence in controlling their use of alcohol and related offending behaviour;
- make different choices and use their experiences as learning tools; and
- examine the consequences of offending and reduce their offending.

AEPS has been shown to play a significant role in managing and reducing risks posed by participants. The AEPS programme is agreed within the framework of a probation supervision action plan and is also used to monitor compliance with the probation order. Sacro staff work in collaboration with supervising social workers who deliver probation orders in Scotland.

By the end of the programme, it is intended that each participant: has a greater understanding of alcohol and its physical and psychological effects; can monitor their own use of alcohol; and has begun to make changes so they feel confident that they can take steps to reduce the likelihood of further alcohol-related offending.

Service users are given clear information about the programme. They are encouraged to give staff their opinions about the service throughout their involvement and give feedback after each programme session. They are required to complete evaluation questionnaires at the end of the programme. Social workers are also involved in the planning, review and completion process.

The programme is delivered in eight weekly sessions, each lasting two hours. The time of the sessions (that is, morning, afternoon or evening) are negotiated with clients to fit in with their other commitments. Gender-specific groups are provided. Each programme accommodates up to eight people; however the women's groups tend to be smaller due to fewer women using the service. Two Sacro workers run the groups. One female worker runs the women-only groups.

Cognitive and behavioural methods of intervention are used. Sessions focus on:

- problem solving;
- self-monitoring;
- risk assessment;
- risk management;
- goal setting;
- consequential thinking;
- strategies of control;
- relapse prevention;
- information giving and sharing – alcohol and drug use;
- cartooning – offence focus; and
- behaviour change and maintenance.

The sessions encourage clients to address and challenge their behaviour. They use a number of techniques including alcohol diaries and sharing experiences. When clients successfully complete the programme, a final meeting is held with the social worker to discuss what has been achieved and to assist future plans. This will lead to a Sacro report that highlights the client's progress, change in attitude, their ability to employ control strategies and any continuing areas of concern. Courts and social workers can have access to this report.

Client numbers in the last year

The service aims to provide 75 programme places per year. Between April 2006 and March 2007, the programme had 143 referrals with:

- 64 from the Sheriff Court (see glossary);
- 18 from social enquiry report authors;
- 60 from supervising officers; and
- 1 from Sacro.

Table 3.1. Number of referrals by referral source, age, sex and ethnic origin

Referral source	Sheriff Court	SER author	Supervising officer	Sacro		
	64	18	60	1		
Age	Under 18	18–21	22–25	26–29	30–39	40+
	6	25	17	24	37	34
Sex	Male	Female				
	125	18				
Ethnic origin	White	Black Caribbean	Black African	Black Other	Asian	Other ethnic origin
	139	0	0	2	0	2

A total of 116 assessments were made between April 2006 and March 2007.

Table 3.2. Number of assessments by age, sex and ethnic origin

Age	Under 18	18–21	22–25	26–29	30–39	40+
	3	21	14	20	30	28
Sex	Male	Female				
	101	15				
Ethnic origin	White	Black Caribbean	Black African	Black Other	Asian	Other ethnic origin
	113	0	0	1	0	2

A total of 90 referrals were assessed as suitable for the programme between April 2006 and March 2007.

Table 3.3. Number of suitable assessments by age, sex and ethnic origin

Age	Under 18	18–21	22–25	26–29	30–39	40+
	2	19	11	15	21	22
Sex	Male	Female				
	80	10				
Ethnic origin	White	Black Caribbean	Black African	Black Other	Asian	Other ethnic origin
	87	0	0	1	0	2

A total of 26 referrals were assessed as unsuitable for the programme between April 2006 and March 2007.

Table 3.4. Number of unsuitable assessments by age, sex and ethnic origin

Age	Under 18	18–21	22–25	26–29	30–39	40+
	1	2	3	5	11	6
Sex	Male	Female				
	21	5				
Ethnic origin	White	Black Caribbean	Black African	Black Other	Asian	Other ethnic origin
	26	0	0	0	0	0
Reason not suitable	Level of drinking	Motivation	Doesn't need service	Group phobia	Other alcohol service more appropriate	
	1	13	5	1	6	

A total of 79 referrals were disposed to the programme between April 2006 and March 2007. This included a total of 55 clients attending as part of a condition of their order.

Table 3.5. Number of disposals by age, sex and ethnic origin

Age	Under 18	18–21	22–25	26–29	30–39	40+
	2	15	10	14	19	19
Sex	Male	Female				
	69	10				
Ethnic origin	White	Black Caribbean	Black African	Black Other	Asian	Other ethnic origin
	76	0	0	1	0	2

A total of 58 clients started the programme between April 2006 and March 2007, including 43 clients as part of their order.

Table 3.6. Number of starters by age, sex and ethnic origin

Age	Under 18	18–21	22–25	26–29	30–39	40+
	1	10	10	9	13	15
Sex	Male	Female				
	49	9				
Ethnic origin	White	Black Caribbean	Black African	Black Other	Asian	Other ethnic origin
	56	0	0	0	0	2

A total of 53 clients completed the programme between April 2006 and March 2007, including 40 clients as part of their order.

Table 3.7. Number of completers by age, sex and ethnic origin

Age	Under 18	18–21	22–25	26–29	30–39	40+
	1	9	9	8	11	15
Sex	Male	Female				
	46	7				
Ethnic origin	White	Black Caribbean	Black African	Black Other	Asian	Other ethnic origin
	51	0	0	0	0	2

A total of four clients did not complete the programme between April 2006 and March 2007 (see next page).

Table 3.8. Number of non-completers by age, sex and ethnic origin

Age	Under 18	18-21	22-25	26-29	30-39	40+
	0	1	0	0	2	1

Sex	Male	Female
	4	0

Ethnic origin	White	Black Caribbean	Black African	Black Other	Asian	Other ethnic origin
	4	0	0	0	0	

Reasons didn't complete	Non attendance	Motivation	Unavoidable circumstances	Behaviour	Other	Illness
	1	0	0	2	0	1

Staffing

AEPS is a very small team of three people: a service manager, team leader and criminal justice worker. In addition, the team recruits and trains sessional workers to help run the groups.

Benefits of the scheme

AEPS provides a non-judgmental and educational service to clients. Its focus on alcohol fills a widely accepted gap. Services that are available focus on health and counselling, rather than offending behaviour.

Sacro shares information with partner agencies, in particular, social services and courts. Keeping courts up-to-date about the service and its outcomes enables courts to increase their confidence in the service and know exactly what it does. Sentencers are also encouraged to give their views on the programme and are invited to complete an annual evaluation questionnaire.

Monitoring, evaluation and effectiveness

At the beginning of each session, clients are invited to provide feedback on the previous session, and this focuses on group dynamics, individual participation and group work practice. This feedback is immediately used to inform future planning. At the final session, clients complete an evaluation form, which is used to shape future development of the service.

If clients cannot attend a particular session they must contact both Sacro staff and their social worker. Sacro staff will also inform social workers of absences or exclusions from any session. Sacro also records issues like alcohol or drug use. If a client misses a group session, arrangements are usually made for them to cover the issues in an individual session. If poor attendance persists, a review meeting is arranged to discuss the client's future participation in AEPS. This is an inclusive process involving the client, Sacro staff and their social worker. Should an exclusion result, the social worker has to inform the court.

AEPS has been evaluated internally and externally. Between May 2000 and December 2002, Elizabeth Cutting evaluated the programme (Cutting 2004). She found that AEPS did succeed in reducing the frequency of reconviction. There was clear reduction in the number of people who were convicted of further offences after completing the AEPS programme. Those who fully competed AEPS had a higher success rate than those who did not (64%), however almost one-half (48%) of those who attended part of a programme, were not reconvicted in the two-year period following the programme.

An internal Sacro evaluation in 2006 (Sacro 2006) concluded that the service provided an appropriate, important, effective and well-used programme for addressing alcohol-related offending in the community. AEPS enhanced existing probation provision by enabling clients to be critical of their own behaviour and challenge each other in a safe group context. The ability to provide gender-specific programmes further encouraged positive personal change while ultimately helping to ensure community safety. Collaborative working, with partner agencies and clients, helped to ensure that AEPS responded well to each of their needs.

Policies

Sacro has all of the policies that one would associated with a large national voluntary organisation that reports to the Scottish Executive, the Care Commission and that has attained both Investors In People (see glossary) and Practical Quality Assurance System for Small Organisations (PQASSO) (see glossary). These policies are comprehensive and they are put into practice through regular service and project review. Additionally, staff attend core training for all criminal justice staff and additional training as identified within annual personal development appraisal plans.

Contact details:

Alastair Cattanach
Programme Manager
Alcohol Education Probation Programme
Sacro
Community Links Centre
Epworth Halls
25 Nicolson Square
Edinburgh

EH8 9BX

Tel: 0131 622 7500

Email: acattanach@lothiancjs.sacro.org.uk

Another Way Service, Sacro, Edinburgh

Scheme of special merit award 2007

A client's experience

The Another Way Service first met 'Zoe' in 2006. She was 24 years old and used heroin and street benzodiazepines every day. When heroin was unavailable she would use dihydrocodeine (see glossary) and occasionally crack cocaine. Zoe had previously received a prescription for methadone through a homeless agency but she had lost her motivation and stopped using the prescription. She funded her drug use by street sex work.

In April 2006, her partner had been on a drug treatment and testing order for nine months without providing a drug-free sample. Zoe acknowledged that her own drug misuse was affecting her partner's motivation to stop using drugs and she agreed to a referral to the Community Drug Problems Service. This meant she had to register with a GP, then to wait several months for an assessment. During this time, Zoe's motivation dwindled and she reported using more heroin than usual. Her assessment eventually took place in July and she was put back on a methadone prescription.

The following month, Sacro met with and started working with Zoe. Various options and ideas were explored. One option was to find training, to fill her time and give her skills. Zoe showed enthusiasm for learning about computing. By the end of the month she was enrolled on, and attending, a college course in IT. Through attending the course, it transpired Zoe needed help with reading and writing, so Sacro arranged literacy support. However the college course eventually proved too much for Zoe and she gave it up.

Zoe had another opportunity, in the shape of a course run by Marks & Spencer. She took part in three weeks' training in one of their stores. Zoe successfully completed the training but it did not lead to the job offer as she had hoped.

*In March 2007, Zoe was given a six-month deferred sentence for the
one outstanding charge against her. With the help and support of the
Another Way Service she has now given up street sex working and
no longer 'tops up' her prescription with street drugs. Her methadone
dosage has been adjusted and she is also receiving medication for her
anxiety and depression. She has received treatment for her physical
health problems and is currently attending two agencies, which are
helping her improve her chances of finding suitable employment.*

Service provider

See page 86.

Origins of the programme

Street prostitution in Edinburgh is a long-established
phenomenon that has been a source of public concern
and controversy; however, there are actually relatively few
women charged with such offences at any one time. In a
12-month period in 2003/04 (Sacro 2007a), police made
73 reports to the procurator fiscal (see glossary) about 28
separate women, while between 1 January and 24 December
2004, 44 reports were submitted about 15 women.

It appears that a small group of women is involved in
street prostitution at any time; however, the make-up of the
group is not constant. In the vast majority of cases women
appear to become involved in street prostitution to finance
their own drug use or, sometimes, that of a friend, relative
or partner. Information suggests that women who engage
in sex work and who are drug dependent have chaotic
lifestyles. Attempts to change their lives often seem to be
hindered by a mistrust of professionals, a reluctance to
engage with services, low self-esteem and poor mental and
physical health. While the number of women using the
Another Way Service is relatively small, the support they
need requires considerable input.

The Another Way Service was initially a 12-month pilot that started in June 2005. It employed one person for 21 hours per week to encourage drug-using street sex workers to engage with drug treatment and care services. The aim was to help women leave prostitution and lead more positive lifestyles.

Funding

The City of Edinburgh and Midlothian Councils are funding the Another Way Service as part of Sacro's Arrest Referral Service (see glossary) until 31 March 2008. It is funded as a pilot, therefore future funding depends on the approval of the Community Justice Authority. Sacro has sought funding up to March 2011.

The Criminal Justice Social Work departments of the two local authorities also provide funding via the local Alcohol and Drug Action Teams.

Support is also provided by stakeholder agencies and they are represented on the steering group. Stakeholder agencies include the police, ScotPEP (Scottish Prostitutes' Education Project), Edinburgh District Court (in the form of a Justice of the Peace and a Clerk of the Court) and the procurator fiscal's office.

The service currently costs £20,000 per annum.

Target group

Women sex workers who have a drug problem can use the Another Way Service. They have to be resident in the City of Edinburgh or Midlothian.

Sacro works in partnership with the City of Edinburgh Council, Justices of the Peace and Clerks of the Court to ensure that there is a variety of entry routes into the service.

The aim is to maximise the opportunities to engage with a hard-to-reach group.

The primary entry route into the service is via a deferred sentence from Edinburgh District Court. The Another Way Service enables the court to defer sentences on women found guilty of prostitution offences for a period of three months (which may be extended) while she engages with the service.

The procurator fiscal can also make referrals as a diversion from prosecution. This has happened where the woman has no previous convictions for prostitution and there is little or no criminal record. The service will also accept referrals from other support agencies and self-referrals.

What does the programme do?

The Another Way Service provides a support and referral service to drug-using street sex workers facing prosecution for prostitution in Edinburgh. As financing a drug habit is the most common reason for involvement in street sex work, the service aims to encourage women to engage with drug treatment and other services and, if possible, to leave prostitution.

The service aims to:

- explore possible options for engaging drug users in drug treatment services;
- help the individuals concerned to access appropriate treatment and care;
- improve the health, safety and welfare of the women concerned and reduce the pressure on them to engage in street sex work and ultimately to stop;
- reduce the number of arrests for street sex work-related offences;

- reduce the number of prosecutions and court appearances for street sex work-related offences; and
- reduce the number of women sentenced for street sex work-related offences.

As many women are referred to the service from court, Another Way Service staff are based at Edinburgh District Court to assess and interview potential service users. A more detailed assessment takes place within the seven days following the court appearance.

The Justice of the Peace defers sentence for three months, therefore initial plans will be made for this period. Another Way Service staff will then report progress or difficulties to the court at the end of this period; the court will then decide whether the sentence should be deferred for longer or whether to take another course of action.

The service provides information and advice about treatment services, harm reduction measures and a wide variety of health, housing, employment and social services relevant to women (and potentially men) working in the street sex industry. It is recognised as both a pathway into treatment and out of prostitution, therefore the service often spends much energy making referrals to specialist agencies. The service's strength lies in its ability to work with and build trusting professional relationships with often hard-to-reach service users.

Women working with the Another Way Service will address issues like low self-esteem and putting previous relapses or negative experiences into context. It will also support them to structure their time so that they can attend appointments, as well as to sustain contact and maintain contact with other agencies.

Client visit protocol

Normally service workers will meet clients at the client's home, in the Community Links Centre (Sacro's office in Edinburgh) or at another agency, as other agencies' staff will be involved.

Client numbers in the last year

In October 2006, the service was working with 15 clients, between the ages of 22 and 38 years. The size of the caseload varies. At the end of 2007 there were 11 live cases. Five of these required only occasional contact and the remaining six had at least weekly contact with the service.

Staffing

The Another Way Service employs one service worker who manages the service on a daily basis. This service is managed alongside two other Sacro services, the Arrest Referral Service and Supervised Bail Service. The team leader for all three of these services supervises the Another Way Service worker.

A steering group guides the Another Way Service's development.

Preventing reoffending

The service aims to reduce the extent to which clients are involved in street sex work, therefore information about their activity comes from the clients themselves. Service users are regularly asked about how often they are working the streets, to provide information over time. Similarly, staff ask service users about their drug use. In this way the relationships between sex working and drug use can be monitored.

The Another Way Service has worked with 15 street sex workers in its first two years. Five of these women have successfully left street sex working with another two reporting that they only engage in prostitution occasionally. Of the 15 women, ten have successfully accessed and used methadone prescriptions.

The Another Way Service closed four cases. Two of the women have referred themselves back to the service when they felt they needed additional support. This reflects Sacro's understanding that women working in the sex industry need consistently high levels of support over a long period of time.

Evaluation and effectiveness

Since the service started in July 2005, there have been two evaluation reports. These reports included interviews with service users, the procurator fiscal's office, the police, the local council and other stakeholder agencies. The aim was to evaluate the service's effectiveness and to assess its impact in terms of improving service users' quality of life and drug misuse.

The evaluations have shown that this model is successful as it provides courts with an actual alternative to fines or imprisonment as well as providing women with an opportunity to get drug treatment and support. It is noteworthy that in relation to prescribing services such as the Harm Reduction Team (HRT), that staff within the HRT have commented that the high success rate of referrals from Another Way Service accessing a methadone prescription appears to result from the intense support that Another Way Service provides around supporting service users to access such services.

The 2007 evaluation report noted that since inception the service has exceeded all expectations, and drawn positive comments from service users, healthcare services, drug services, specialist services for sex workers, and also from Justices of the Peace and Clerks of the Court. For example one clerk said:

The District Court Justices and Legal Assessors have been very pleased to be associated with the Another Way Project since its inception in 2005. It has greatly assisted the Court to have another sentencing option, which specifically aims to deal with the problems underlying these offences and offenders. The Court has also been pleased to see from the reports provided that rehabilitation is being successfully achieved in several cases. If the Project ceases to exist the Court will be deprived of an extremely useful sentencing option and the Accused will lose the benefit of the intensive rehabilitation work, which the Project has been able to carry out.

Deirdre Morrison
Clerk of the Court, Edinburgh District Court

Contact details:

Chris Wheeldon
Service Manager, Sacro Another Way Service
Sacro Community Links Centre
25 Nicholson Square
Edinburgh
EH8 9BX

Tel: 0131 622 7500

Email: info@lothiancjs.sacro.org.uk

Domestic Abuse Group (DAG), Sacro, Falkirk

Outstanding scheme award 2007

A client's experience

'Andy' was sentenced to probation following his third assault conviction against his partner, 'Sally'. He had long regarded violence as a functional, acceptable way to resolve conflict, in all areas of his life and his behaviour was exacerbated by alcohol.

Andy was suspended from his DAG placement as he failed to attend the first four sessions but he was given another chance. After the first few sessions he became a positive and influential group member. He took advantage of the process-driven 'update' at the start of each group where he was urged to examine his behaviour in the past week.

Andy was often asked to lead the way in new exercises due to his willingness to take responsibility for his abusive behaviour and to look at what he needed to do to change it. He adopted a very positive approach to the most difficult exercises, such as the offence account and the victim empathy exercise. He focused on what he would gain by completing them rather than thinking of how hard it would be, or giving self-justifying responses.

During his offence account he moved from providing a passive account of his behaviour to being able to identify the thoughts and feelings that lead him to be violent and abusive. Andy told the group: 'I felt Sally was in control. I felt like a kid being told where to go. I was feeling unappreciated'. The group work gave him a better understanding of how Sally might have felt. He acknowledged that Sally would have been scared that I would get lifted (arrested), or seriously hurt. She'd have been scared that I'd kick off again and assault her.

By the end of the group Andy had completed a comprehensive relapse prevention plan. While Andy attended the DAG programme, Sacro's women's services worker supported Sally. She was very positive about the changes Andy made.

*Eighteen months after Andy completed the DAG programme, Sally
told Sacro: I definitely feel safer, he's changed. Andy doesn't storm off
angry, he talks things through. The women's service was helpful because
it was confidential. I was able to discuss problems without involving
the police.*

Service provider

See page 86.

Type of programme

Sacro's Domestic Abuse Group (DAG) is part of an
intervention system that works in partnership with the
local criminal justice services. It aims to reduce the risk
of violence and abuse to women and their children. Men
who have been found guilty of violent or abusive offences
against a current or former partner attend the DAG. They
must have shown a willingness to address it. The men are
challenged to explore their abusive behaviours to help them
take more control over their actions, thereby preventing
further abuse.

Origins of the programme

Police statistics (Sacro 2007b) showed 45,796 detected
incidents of domestic abuse in Scotland during 2005/06.
In 87% of cases, domestic abuse was committed by a man
against a women. Fifty-five per cent of cases involved repeat
victimisation. However, only 52% of incidents led to the
recording of an offence.

Other evidence from the Scottish Crime Survey in 2007
(Davidson and Whyte 2007) showed that 6% of women had
been threatened, and 5% had force used against them, by
their partner or ex-partner, in the previous year. Of those
affected by domestic abuse in the previous year, only 34%
informed the police of an incident where force was used

against them. This information suggested that domestic abuse – particularly the victimisation of women by men – was a major problem in Scotland and that there needed to be interventions designed to work with the men who commit domestic abuse against women.

Sacro's programme was an attempt to provide a credible community-based disposal for people convicted of domestic abuse, who would previously have received a short prison sentence, community service or a fine. None of these sentences forced the man to take responsibility for his behaviour. Sacro drew from their existing programmes and adopted a multi-modal approach, using cognitive behavioural work, pro-social modelling and psychodrama.

Sacro has provided DAG programmes in Forth Valley for the last nine years.

Funding

Three local authorities, Falkirk (the principal funder), Stirling and Clackmannanshire provide a criminal justice social work grant to support this programme. The associated services staff are funded through the Scottish Executive 'Violence Against Women' programme until March 2008 with the purpose of developing the services.

Target group

Men convicted of offences involving domestic abuse. Support is also given to their partners, ex-partners and children where appropriate. Men are sentenced to attend the programme either as an alternative to a custodial sentence or as an additional requirement to a custodial sentence.

What does the programme do?

DAG aims to:

- offer a structured personal change programme for male domestic abuse perpetrators, in partnership with criminal justice services;
- provide a structured environment where service users can explore their domestically abusive behaviour and its impact on themselves and others, with a view to encouraging positive, achievable change; and
- place the safety of women and children at the forefront of any work undertaken with men by providing a comprehensive support service to female partners and ex-partners of service users that links with the men's programme.

Using group work, DAG seeks to:

- enable group members to understand the nature of their domestic abuse by making links between their thoughts, feelings and their actions;
- challenge, as appropriate, service users' beliefs, attitudes and distorted thinking;
- develop group members' capacity to accept responsibility for their own behaviour;
- enable service users to understand their own cycle of abusive behaviour so that they may exercise more control over it;
- increase group members' victim awareness and empathy by examining the consequences of their own and others' abusiveness;
- assist group members to identify potential high-risk situations and to construct a realistic relapse prevention strategy for themselves;

- liaise regularly with the women's services worker to ensure that women have accurate information regarding the programme, men's attendance on the programme and to share information where appropriate;
- provide regular feedback regarding service users' progress to their supervising officer and sentencers;
- to provide supervision, risk assessment and risk management of service users attending the programme; and
- work in partnership with the police Domestic Abuse Unit.

Sacro has found that men are generally apprehensive about attending a domestic abuse group. Generally they do not see themselves as 'wife beaters' and feel high levels of guilt and shame about their abusive behaviour. They are often sceptical about the possibility of change. Sacro believes that the pre-group stage of the programme is crucial in engaging the man and providing knowledge and 'tools' to believe change is possible. A motivational approach is used.

Figure 3.9. The Domestic Abuse Group programme

Sessions	Aim of activity and outcomes
Pre-group sessions	
Weeks 1-3	Increase motivation to engage with case manager. Explore own experiences and beliefs. Demonstrate listening skills.
Weeks 4-7	Increase awareness of behaviour. Increase belief in changing behaviour. Explore obstacles to achieving this
Induction sessions	
Weeks 1-4	Explore hopes and fears of the group. Formulate group rules. Look at men's rationalisation of behaviour.
Weeks 5-11	Take responsibility for abusive behaviour. Write offence accounts, which are shared with the group. Group ask further questions of each account to illicit further information and increase accountability. Focus on cognitive processes underlying offending behaviour.
Weeks 12-15	Look at victim awareness, develop empathy and look at reparation. Role modelling of offender, partner, victim (child or relative) in turn and answering questions according to each role and being challenged by the group on how each person feels and would say about the situation.
Weeks 16-17	Increase understanding and process of offending, looking at how each member feels, thinks and behaves. Explore how to recognise moods and emotions and early warning signals. Look at benefits of a relationship based on equality rather then power and control.

	Practice skills needed to avoid abusive behaviour.
	Skills practice designed for each member focusing on individual identified needs.
Weeks 18-20	Complete a relapse prevention plan – looking at high-risk moods, situations, coping mechanisms.
	Have personal support network in place.

The number of weeks that the programme takes to complete varies depending on whether the programme is delivered during the day or in the evening. Generally the day programme takes 24 weeks to complete.

Sacro offers the women partners, ex-partners and their children, support services including advocacy, support, risk management, safety planning as well as information about the DAG and their partners' attendance. This service is tailor made and will generally take place in a community setting or their home. This service can be sought without the men knowing. Sacro regards close communication between DAG group workers and those working with their partners as essential to reducing the men's risk of perpetrating more abuse. The women are regarded as 'consultants' to help understand their partners' abusive behaviour.

Client visit protocol

Staff undertaking home visits are required to log into a monitoring system. Using their mobile phones staff provide an address for the visit and an expected departure time. Should a staff member fail to log off and fail to respond to two text 'prompts', the police are notified and asked to attend the address. Men sign agreements not to be at home when Sacro staff visit their partners and children if they are aware of their participation in the programme.

Client numbers in the last year

Sacro aims to deliver DAG programmes each year. Services for partners and their children are available on a year-round basis. Between 2002 and 2006, 13 DAG programmes have been completed. During this time, 112 people started the programme, of whom 63 people completed. Each programme has eight people start in the group. This is a completion rate of 56%. The reasons for not completing the programme have included: a failure to attend; personal circumstances changing like moving away; being convicted of a further offence and returning to court or custody; not being able to cope with the pressure of being on the group; and subsequently being breached by their supervising officer.

There were 21 women using the women's service during 2004/05, 37 during 2005/06, and 41 during 2006/07.

Monitoring

Sacro has developed a database to monitor referrals and attendance on the programme alongside their client's personal details like age and their offence. Service users also complete a feedback form at the end of each group session to assess their views in terms of attitude. At the end of the programme both the service user and their partner complete questionnaires that include behavioural checklists.

Staffing

The programme has an operations manager to oversee the work with the support of the service manager and a service team leader who are both part-time. A team of group workers and associated service workers deliver the programme. The project has a steering group chaired by the service manager for the Criminal Justice Social Work

Department in Falkirk. The service managers for criminal justice social work in Clackmannanshire and Stirling also attend.

Benefits of the scheme

Many partners have reported to Sacro that the primary benefit of the programme, for them, is the reduction in abusive behaviour and a change in the men's attitude. The following testimony from those involved with DAG highlight the benefits:

I believe that this project provides men with a safe space to consider the feelings, thoughts, beliefs and attitudes which underpin their abusive behaviour. It also provides them with the tools to effect positive changes. As importantly, our work with women helps them to manage their risk more effectively and to keep themselves and their children safe.

DAG programme manager

An amazing, humbling experience which can change you into a much better person if you want to make those changes. Rewarding, challenging, I wish I'd made the changes long before now.

A service user

Whatever he's learning from the group, he appears to be facing up to his behaviour. He appears to be learning to keep himself safe. There was someone for me to talk to. [My partner] also saw the difference in me as I was no longer isolated and he could not use my previous isolation as a weapon against me.

A service user's partner

Diversity, policies in place

In addition to the Sacro policies outlined in the AEPS section above, staff work to the standards laid out by Respect, the UK-wide professional association for domestic abuse work programmes and associated services, which include policies relating to diversity.

Contact details:

Simon McLean,
Service Manager, Sacro Falkirk
22 Meeks Road
Falkirk
FK2 7ET

Tel: 01324 627821

Email: info@falkirk.sacro.org.uk

CHAPTER 4

Restorative Justice and Mediation

Restorative justice provides opportunities for those directly affected by an offence as a victim of crime, as a perpetrator of an offence or as a member of the wider community, to communicate and agree on how to deal with the offence and its consequences.

The restorative justice process allows victims the chance to tell offenders the real impact of the crime, to get answers to their questions and to receive an apology. It also gives the perpetrators a chance to understand the impact of their actions and to do something to repair the harm they have caused. Therefore restorative justice holds offenders directly accountable for their actions and can help victims get on with their lives.

Research shows that restorative justice works best when it deals with crimes where there is an identifiable victim who may meet with the offender. An aim of restorative justice and mediation is to enhance victim satisfaction, reduce their fear of crime and to make amends for the harm that has been done to them. For the perpetrators, restorative justice helps them to increase their awareness of the consequences of crime and their actions, provides an opportunity to make reparation and help to reintegrate them back into their community. Restorative justice community programmes can also be regarded as a tool to enhance public confidence, particularly when they include visible and reparative work in the local area.

Restorative justice programmes and their ethos are now firmly embedded in the criminal justice system's response to adults and young people and are regarded as effective (Shapland et al. 2004, 2006; Sherman and Strang 2007).

The Howard League for Penal Reform's Community Programmes Awards have recognised work undertaken with both adults and young people: Remedi with adults and the Suffolk Reparation and Mediation Service with young people. They are both examples of professionally-run schemes with committed staff that demonstrate a real clarity of purpose. Both schemes are really solidly embedded in their communities with a strong use of volunteers. Their strength also lies in the ability to individually tailor the process to meet the needs of all parties to achieve the best possible solutions and outcomes.

Remedi – Victim Offender Mediation Service (Adult), South Yorkshire

Scheme of special merit award 2005

Service provider

Remedi is an independent charity, which offers a full range of restorative justice services across South Yorkshire. It specialises in adult mediation. Its aims are to provide a mediation service that allows victims to express their needs and offenders to take responsibility for their actions.

Remedi began in Sheffield in 1996. Home Office research funding was secured in Spring 2001, which allowed expansion across South Yorkshire. Remedi is now a company limited by guarantee and a registered charity.

Funding

The scheme is funded through the South Yorkshire Probation Area, the South Yorkshire YOT (see glossary), the Esmée Fairbairn Foundation, Neighbourhood Renewal, the Community Fund, Community Safety Partnership and the Children's Fund (see glossary). All these funds are time limited. Remedi also has funding from the Home Office for research.

South Yorkshire Probation Area funds Remedi's victim awareness work.

Referrals

Remedi takes referrals directly from individuals or agencies. The majority are self-referrals generated from information in prison contained in probation resettlement packs. Referrals also come from probation officers, probation victim contact officers and the police.

What does the programme do?

Mediation involves communication between the victim of the crime and the person who committed it. Mediators act as go-betweens to enable communication between the two parties. The process is entirely voluntary, taking as many meetings as necessary before proceeding to mediation or closing the case. People are free to opt out at any time. If both the victim and offender wish, a face-to-face meeting can be arranged.

The Victim Offender Mediation Service offers mediation only if the offender accepts responsibility for the crime. Only then will mediators seek consent from the victim(s) to proceed with contact between the two parties.

Fully trained mediators will work in pairs. They will talk with the perpetrator about the offence, their attitude to victims and what they expect from mediation. Rigorous assessments are carried out to ensure that mediation is a suitable option.

Mediation can be either direct or indirect:

- Direct – when a victim and an offender decide to meet face-to-face, in a safe, neutral venue and in the presence of mediators.
- Indirect – when a mediator acts as a go-between, relaying information (either verbally or through a letter) between the victim and the offender.

Mediation may also include reparation, where a specific action is carried out by the offender at the request of the victim. The aim is to make amends for the harm caused by the offence.

Mediation can take place at any stage in the criminal justice process provided that:

- the offender accepts responsibility for the crime;
- both the victim and the offender are willing to participate; and
- mediators consider it to be safe emotionally and physically for those involved to participate.

If a case proceeds to direct mediation, both parties will sign an agreement. This will outline the amount of information each party is happy to disclose to the other. Mediation can be stopped at any point in the process by either party. At this point both parties will receive a letter to advise that the process is being brought to a close. Remedi staff will always undertake a final follow-up visit.

Where indirect mediations have taken place, participants are asked to complete a questionnaire. However, where cases are particularly complicated, staff will visit each party.

In addition, Remedi has developed a range of resources to deliver victim awareness work for South Yorkshire Probation Area and YOT. It is used where there is no identifiable victim or where a victim chooses not to engage in mediation. Remedi also delivers the programme for youth offender panels and in prisons. Resources have been developed that focus on car crime, shoplifting, drug-related crime, violent crime and burglary. As a part of this process letters of apology may be written that can be passed on to the victims of crime should they wish to receive them.

One-to-one victim awareness training sessions are delivered to adults subject to either a community sentence or released on licence from prison. These referrals come through the probation service. Using the individual's experience as a springboard, the sessions will explore:

- the concepts of 'direct' and 'indirect' victims, and harm;
- an appreciation of the harm caused to their victim(s) and the general impact of their crime; and
- what restorative justice could mean for them.

Group victim awareness sessions have been developed for the probation service. It is part of a ten-week programme delivered in partnership with the probation service.

Remedi tries to ensure that it is an inclusive process. As mediators generally work in pairs it is possible to ensure that all participants are comfortable and feel supported. This can be achieved by a male and female mediator working together, or matching mediators based on race, or class. Remedi also employs translators where necessary and have French speaking mediators as part of their team.

Client numbers

In the year ending October 2007, Remedi worked with 127 adult referrals and 358 youth referrals. They contacted 763 victims of crime, 90% of whom participated in mediation. Information from Remedi suggests that 98% were satisfied with the outcome of their mediation.

Staffing

Remedi is a company limited by guarantee and a registered charity. It has 45 members, all with one vote each and this membership includes organisations and individuals. The board of trustees has seven members including senior probation staff, magistrates, a solicitor and academics.

There are six full-time senior staff members and a further 18 members of staff consisting of full-time staff and sessional staff. In addition there are 17 fully trained volunteers.

Staff have regular supervisions with line managers. In addition there is a county-wide supervisory board that provides additional support to staff and volunteers. It acts as a monitoring tool but also a vehicle to enhance staff knowledge.

Benefits of the programme

Victims are central to Remedi's work. However this does not preclude effective working with the perpetrators of crime. Both are given the chance to resolve issues, feel empowered, have their say, move on and have a sense of satisfaction.

Victims of crime can be left feeling angry and fearful. Their lives can be disrupted for a long time after the event. Mediation offers the chance for them to:

- have questions answered;
- explore feelings resulting from the crime;
- tell the offender how the crime has affected them;
- receive an apology;
- ask the offender to make amends in some way; and
- reduce the fear of crime and further victimisation.

Equally, offenders can be left feeling remorseful and wanting to find a way to put the offence behind them. Mediation offers them opportunities to:

- take responsibility for their actions;
- explain why they did it;
- confront the effects of their offending on the victim;
- apologise; and
- make amends.

The communities where crimes happen can be left feeling vulnerable, fearful and helpless. The range of intervention delivered by Remedi can allow the community to see a direct and constructive response to crime and an opportunity for reparation. Ultimately it may help reduce fear of crime in the community.

Volunteers

Remedi uses volunteers to support its mediation work. Potential volunteers complete an application form and then they will be interviewed. Police checks are made on all staff and volunteers.

Full training is given to all volunteers. There are six, three-hour sessions and a residential weekend course to complete. However training is ongoing throughout a volunteer's time with Remedi.

All out-of-pocket expenses are paid to volunteers.

Support is provided to volunteers through regular mediators' meetings at which casework will be discussed and outside speakers are invited to develop volunteers' knowledge base.

Volunteers may also accompany and observe experienced mediators on cases. Regular supervision meetings are held with staff.

Evaluation and effectiveness

At the beginning and the end of the process, participants are invited to evaluate the service and to express their opinions about mediation and their motivations for taking part.

Evaluations have shown that offenders are grateful for the opportunity to try to make amends and move on in their lives to a different future:

Very worthwhile and got me to think about my actions and the trouble it caused to the victim.

Mediation has made a very big difference. It has made my goal stronger and given me more determination to succeed in life and never commit crime again.

Post-mediation quotes from offenders

Staff evaluations of direct mediation emphasise the qualitative nature of the process. Staff explained that not all of the work results can be quantified as it is very difficult to put down on paper how people are affected by the process.

Since 2001, the University of Sheffield evaluated Remedi for the Home Office (Shapland *et al.* 2004, 2006). The results have been positive, with both victims and offenders finding the process useful and satisfactory.

Contact details:

Remedi South Yorkshire Head Office
Scotia Works
Leadmill Road
Sheffield
S1 4SE

Tel: 0114 2412795

Email: sheffield@remediuk.org

Suffolk Reparation and Mediation Service (SRAMS), Crime Concern

Outstanding scheme award 2005

A client's experience

'Stephen' was 15 years old when he was referred to the SRAMS by SYOT as part of a 12-month referral order with a 29-hour contract. The order followed conviction for criminal damage at three local community sites. He undertook reparation work directly in line with the victim's wishes and letters of apology were written.

Stephen worked on a conservation site to make the site accessible to all community members. This encouraged Stephen to take responsibility for his actions by explaining and apologising for his behaviour and paying back directly to those he had offended against. He was able to gain a clearer understanding of the consequences of his actions with the added benefit of encouraging him to become part of the local community.

Service provider

Crime Concern's reparation and mediation project is a fully integrated restorative justice service which complements the work of Suffolk Youth Offending Team (SYOT). Crime Concern is a charity that has been working to reduce crime and create safer communities in England and Wales since 1988.

Origins of the programme

The SYOT wanted to expand and develop its reparation work with young people so put out tenders. Crime Concern won the bid. The current scheme has been running since 2003. It is based within SYOT.

Funding

SRAMS receives funding from SYOT.

Target group

Any young person aged 10 to 17 years who has committed an offence. Referrals to SRAMS are made through SYOT following a court appearance or after attending a youth offender panel. The project receives around 50 referrals a month and on average each young person carries out between 10 and 12 hours of reparation per week.

What does the programme do?

SRAMS is a countywide project with offices in Ipswich, Bury St Edmunds and Lowestoft. SRAMS is an inclusive project that works with young people to find appropriate ways for them to repay their local community for the offences they have committed. The project allows young people, though restorative justice techniques, to acknowledge the consequences of their actions and provide opportunities to make amends that are valued in the community. The scheme encourages service users to take responsibility for their actions. It also gives victims of crime a voice as they may have the opportunity to ask questions, hear the young person's views and put a face to the perpetrator of the crime. The SRAMS model asks community projects to provide their clients with direct reparative tasks.

SRAMS delivers:

- victim offender mediation;
- shuttle mediation (staff relay the messages and wishes of the victim to the offender without direct contact);
- direct reparation in line with the victim's wishes;

- a letter of apology/explanation; and
- community reparation.

The type of work undertaken by SRAMS will depend on participants' wishes; for example, if a victim chooses not to become involved the young person will undertake tasks to benefit the wider community. Most of the activities currently involve SRAMS staff supervising young people to undertake doing reparation in the community. The opportunity for direct mediation is limited but this is a SRAMS development goal.

Once SRAMS is offered an opportunity for other work it will be assessed for suitability. If it is suitable, staff will draw up a programme of work with the community site and reiterate their responsibilities, like ensuring health and safety matters. This forms the basis on which a young person is referred to the site to undertake community reparation

SRAMS staff will identify a young person. An agreement will be drawn up between SRAMS and the young person, which outlines the required standards of behaviour expected from him/her whilst on placement. This supervising officer will then arrange for the placement to go ahead. Young people will only attend sites where they will be treated with respect as SRAMS believes many young people have faced enough rejection throughout their lives.

SRAMS offers total supervision on sites, which means no young person is ever on their own. Staff usually take the young people to and from reparation sites as long distances often have to be travelled to placements. Project staff encourage all young people to learn and get the most out of the experience, and make sure staff have time during the placement to talk to the young people about their crime and the victim.

SRAMS now enjoys strong support from the local community. This is reflected in its strong volunteer base and partnership with 70 reparation placement sites. SRAMS no longer has to search for placements.

A young person's placement depends on an initial assessment. This will lead to decisions based on a young person's educational abilities; training; whether it is beneficial for them to work in a group or alone; and the number of hours of reparation they are required to complete. The young person is encouraged to express opinions about the type of placement they would like.

Examples of placements:

The Wildlife Trust – Young people work with other local volunteers, some with special needs, on conservation sites. This placement encourages the young people to learn to work with, understand, and communicate with, diverse groups of people.

The Genesis Project – This project provides a wide range of care, support and training for people with learning and physical disabilities. Young people on this placement help to decorate the building, learning how to prepare, clean and decorate rooms. Young people also share their breaks with people attending the project, which helps with their communication skills and acceptance of diversity.

Pony riding for the disabled – On this placement young people work with horses, and help to clean and maintain the stables. Young people also act as side riders when disabled people are riding.

Allotments and gardens – Young people helped to clear the garden at an old people's home, and helped to design the new garden layout, with bedding plants and flowers and seating. They worked alongside residents. This placement aims to break down barriers between the young and old and help to develop a sense of community for the young people.

Over time the project has grown and changed. Initially SRAMS staff were cautious about mediation work because of the potential for direct contact between young people and the victims of crime. However, with increasing confidence with the project potential, the amount of direct mediation and face-to-face meetings with victims of crime has increased. This growth has been supported by the introduction of YOT (see glossary) victim liaison officers.

Young people are clearly told what is required of them during their time with SRAMS. They are told that non-co-operation and non-attendance will be reported back to the SYOT. Both the SYOT and SRAMS send warning letters if appointments are missed. SRAMS regards the letter as the vehicle to providing the young person with a second chance. The SYOT sends two warning letters after which they are sent back to court or the youth offender panel.

Client numbers

Table 4.1. Number of young people referred to SRAMS between November 2006 and October 2007, in relation to sex, type of referral case and number of reparation hours

Month	Male	Female	Referral cases*	Restorative justice cases	Reparation cases	Total cases	Total hours
Nov 06	33	15	48			48	654
Dec 06	28	9	37			37	454
Jan 07	21	6		4	23	27	328
Feb 07	32	8		8	32	40	426
Mar 07	26	4		2	28	30	282
Apr 07	27	9		8	28	36	434
May 07	51	12		8	55	63	717
Jun 07	31	10		10	31	41	504
July 07	48	12		12	48	60	659
Aug 07	40	8		12	36	48	510
Sep 07	30	11		12	29	41	433
Oct 07	11	7		4	14	18	196
Total	**378**	**111**	**85**	**80**	**324**	**489**	**5,597**

Note: *SRAMS reporting style was changed in January 2007, with referrals being separated.

Table 4.2. Number of young people referred to SRAMS between November 2006 and October 2007, by sex and ethnic origin

Ethnic origin	Male	Female	Total
White British	358	95	453
Black British	7	7	14
Dual Heritage	9	4	13
Other	3	1	4
Undisclosed	3	2	5
Total	380	109	489

Table 4.3. Number of young people referred to SRAMS between November 2006 and October 2007, by sex and age

Age	Male	Female	Total
10 to 11	4	0	4
11 to 12	7	0	7
12 to 13	16	1	17
13 to 14	37	15	52
14+	316	93	409
Total	380	109	489

Monitoring

SRAMS staff work hard to support young people, thereby reducing the likelihood of breach. Staff complete feedback questionnaires to provide comments on how the order has gone, the young person's general attitude, their attitude to their crime and the standard of their work. Copies of the questionnaire are sent to the YOS. Monthly figures are also submitted to SYOS showing the number of hours completed.

Staffing

The project is staffed by: one full-time manager; five full-time and five part-time reparation and mediation officers; nine sessional workers; and 20 volunteers.

Staff are based in three area offices which cover the whole of Suffolk.

Regular supervision is provided for all staff and there are monthly team meetings.

SRAMS staff adhere to policies set by Crime Concern. All policies are available to view on the organisation's Intranet and in a staff handbook. Each month any new changes that are made are identified on the Intranet and shared with the team at their monthly meetings. Staff reported that this proactive approach works really well, as they feel there is back up all the time and up-to-date information.

Benefits of the scheme

SRAMS believes that the scheme is beneficial to the victims of crime as it enables them, and the wider community, to engage with young people who have committed crimes. Feedback from SRAMS staff shows that people from the placements often give the young people lots of encouragement to stick to their order and to improve their lives.

Project staff are real champions and advocates of restorative justice techniques, which is why they believe the project works so well.

Margaret Miles manages SRAMS. She told the Howard League for Penal Reform:

We see the programme as the way forward when looking for long-term solutions and opportunities within the community for young people who have offended. Service delivery has allowed young people, victims of crime and community members to be actively involved in the criminal justice system, offering opportunities to describe feelings and shape outcomes.

Contact details:

Margaret Miles
Crime Concern Suffolk Programme Manager
Suffolk Reparation and Mediation Service
Crime Concern
c/o Suffolk YOT
45 St Andrews Street South
Bury St Edmunds
IP33 3PH

Tel: 01284 352383

Email: margaret.miles@yots.suffolkcc.gov.uk

CHAPTER 5

Community Sentences and Programmes for Young People

C ommunity sentences and work with community-based programmes can yield good outcomes for young people. The Howard League for Penal Reform's Community Programmes Award winners have shown various ways of working with young people, and have used varying methods including multi-agency and community-based teams to tackle multiple needs.

An overarching theme in these programmes is the importance of being local: to the target group and involving the local community. The local structure of a community programme can also help young people reintegrate into the community. Three of the award winners, the Lodge Hill Challenge, A New Direction Project and White Gold Project particularly demonstrate this. They are targeted multi-modal, multi-disciplinary schemes to work with young people.

The last community programme in this section demonstrates how it is possible to work successfully using a partnership model with disparate and entrenched communities. IMPACT is a joint community-statutory response to car crime in Belfast. The partnership works to develop solutions that will help reduce and prevent car theft within their target area.

Lodge Hill Challenge (LHC), Lodge Hill Trust and West Sussex Youth Offending Service

Outstanding scheme award 2007

A client's experience

'Steve' was 17 years old. He was angry when he arrived at LHC for his compulsory stage 1 session. He thought he would just do stage 1 and walk away.

Steve worked in MacDonald's. He would now describe it as a nondescript job. It was boring but it gave him some money. He felt pressure from his mates to get involved in anti-social and criminal behaviour. His elder brother misused drugs.

At the end of stage 1 Steve began to engage with the programme and volunteered to come back for stage 2. He found the challenges rewarding and enjoyed the teamwork. He also started to question his offending behaviour.

Steve went on to complete all four stages and gained his sports leadership qualification. Lloyds TSB provided sponsorship for Steve to become a trainee activity instructor at Lodge Hill for one year. Through LHC Steve grasped what he described as his second chance and obtained additional skills. He did not want to slide back into his old ways. He became a valued member of the Lodge Hill Team and even returned to the youth offender panel to help with a presentation to them about future referrals to the LHC.

Service provider

The Lodge Hill Trust owns and manages the Lodge Hill Centre. It provides residential, camping and day meeting facilities. The Lodge Hill Trust aims to advance young people's education by helping them to develop their mental and physical capacities, to grow into integrated members of the community. The centre also provides further education facilities for adults.

Origins of the programme

The Lodge Hill Trust recognised that young people at risk of offending and anti-social behaviour were often excluded from participating in social and residential experiences. The LHC was set up in 1999 at the Lodge Hill Centre to provide residential facilities and activities for young people. LHC initially started with a three-stage programme, only introducing the fourth stage when funding was obtained. In 2007 the Trust registered as an access organisation for the Duke of Edinburgh's Award Scheme, giving young people a chance to obtain further training.

Funding

The project is funded by donations from individuals, organisations and various charitable trusts, for example, Lloyds TSB, Horsham District Council and the Bradbury Foundation. There is no statutory funding. A further three years' funding has been secured from 1 April 2007.

Target group

Young people come to the programme as part of a court order or via the local youth sentencing panel. Only stage 1 of the four-stage programme is a compulsory part of a court order. The completion of the other stages is voluntary. It is possible to complete all four stages in a 12-month period.

What does the programme do?

The LHC programme is a partnership with West Sussex Youth Offending Service (WSYOS). It seeks to re-engage young people who are sent via a court order or who are at risk of offending behaviour. The programme works to raise young people's self-esteem and to encourage them to take responsibility for themselves.

The LHC programme is delivered in four stages. It focuses on communication, confidence building and personal development. The scheme also aims to prepare young people to re-engage in education, employment or training. The programme provides a phase to develop group working and citizenship skills; enhance integration and social inclusion; and promote non-criminal activities. It aims to reduce the level and gravity of offending behaviour.

The LHC promotes five core values:

- the personal development of young people and helping them to reach their true potential;
- providing positive social activities by encouraging young people to try new physical challenges and move into new positive community groups;
- developing leadership skills by teaching young people to work with others, improve communication skills and motivate others;
- the change in attitudes and behaviour of young people aiming for alternative positive outcomes; and
- a reduction in the levels of crimes, by providing safe activities and keeping young people out of trouble.

These are achieved via the four-stage programme. Common themes run throughout the stages: communication; confidence building; and, personal development. Stages 1 and 2 take a day to complete while stages 3 and 4 are completed during a weekend residential course.

Stage 1:

This stage is compulsory and lasts for one day. Young people work in groups of 12. The focus is on team working within the grounds of the Lodge Hill Centre. LHC staff report that young people often arrive angry, aggressive and determined not to co-operate. WSYOS trains a team of volunteer mentors to work on the scheme. These are matched with young people as appropriate. At the end of the day young people are invited to continue on the project on a voluntary basis.

Stage 1 begins with an introduction and briefing session highlighting the ground rules and expectations for the day. The participants have to work together in challenging, team-building activities aimed at encouraging them to consider the effect of their actions on others. Activities include high ropes, low ropes, and orienteering challenges. All young people have lunch together to encourage a family dining experience and communication. The afternoon activity involves archery where all young people work to achieve excellence at their own personal level. The day ends with a debrief. At the end of the day young people are invited to continue on the project on a voluntary basis. All young people are also introduced to the Duke of Edinburgh Awards and encouraged to take part.

Stage 2:

This stage uses more difficult and challenging team-building exercises to encourage young people to consider their (potential) offending behaviour.

Stage 3:

This is a two-day residential stage which is often the first time the participants have been away from home. This stage promotes the advantages of working together and the strength of team working. Activities include climbing walls, abseiling, go-karting and paintballing. LHC staff use the time to talk about possible future employment in outdoor activities and the courses, qualifications and apprenticeship that might be available for young people at the final stage.

Stage 4:

The main objectives of this stage is to provide learning and accreditation opportunities to enable young people obtain a recognised qualification in peer education and outdoor education programmes. Young people, aged 16 years and over and who have completed the first three stages, are invited to join the programme. Young people's training needs are identified and a plan of action negotiated. After acceptance on to the programme, young people take part in two-day residential activities to learn group management skills and take part in peer education training.

Once they have completed this, a young person will progress to an individual course. This includes at least two outdoor pursuit courses and a further 20 hours of group tuition at Lodge Hill in order to achieve the Community Sports Leaders Award (see glossary). This takes approximately six days.

Ultimately the LHC provides young people with a peer education programme, work experience and group practice skills.

Client numbers

Approximately 180 young people take part on the programme every year. A young person who completes all four stages will spend 208 hours on the programme as well as additional time with WSYOS.

Table 5.1. Numbers of young people and groups at each stage

Stage	No. of young people in group	No. of groups per year
1	12	12
2	12–14	6
3	16–18	2
4	12	1

Staffing

Lodge Hill provides the staff for the programme. The ratio of staff to young people depends on the size of the group; for example, a group of 12 young people would require three activity instructors, two WSYOS staff and volunteer mentors.

LHC has an advisory committee. It is made up from the Lodge Hill Trust and local partner agencies, including the youth, adult education and social services, primary and secondary schools associations, and the parish council. It also includes two members from the youth cabinet elected to represent the youth parliament for the year. There are four advisory committee meetings per year.

Volunteers

Volunteer mentors are provided by WSYOS to work on the scheme with the young people.

Monitoring and evaluation

Young people complete feedback forms on all stages of the LHC. These can inform change to the course content.

WSYOS uses the Youth Offending Information System (YOIS) which analyses individual factors including health, education, criminal career, accommodation issues, relationships, etc. LHC uses the information it generates too, to assess the level of individual need. WSYOS staff and individual mentors carry out the individual monitoring of young people.

Young people also complete self-esteem and confidence questionnaires at the beginning and end of the project. Their personal adviser will also write a report about what the young person has achieved.

Outcomes

For the last eight years, the LHC's own results show:

- 98% of young people achieve the individual stages;
- WSYOS statistics indicate that 80% of young people either do not go on to offend again or the gravity of their offending is reduced; and
- of the 30% young people not in education, employment or training (NEET), the service provided 80% of these with access to a personal advisor or educational support. It is anticipated that 80% of these young people will move from NEET to EET.

Contact details:

Nick Turner

Activities Manager, Lodge Hill Centre

Watersfield

Pulborough

West Sussex

RH20 1LZ

Tel: 01798 831411

Email: nick@lodgehill.org.uk

A New Direction Project, Sunderland Youth Offending Service and South of Tyne Intensive Surveillance and Supervision Programme (ISSP)

Outstanding scheme award 2007

A client's experience

'Kyle' was 16 years old. He was sentenced to a supervision order with an ISSP for dishonesty offences. He had already been excluded from school. Eventually he was persuaded to get involved with the New Direction Project. The idea was to demonstrate, through working on the project, that he wanted to return into mainstream education.

Kyle's attendance on the New Direction Project was 100%. He enthusiastically embraced a work ethic and showed some talent for painting and wallpapering. He developed a good working relationship with the co-ordinator and went on to complete various decorating jobs in the community, for family and friends. This helped repair some of the relationships that had broken down due to his offending and disruptive behaviour.

His work improved to such an extent that it was decided to use him as a peer mentor within the project. Kyle was offered a return to mainstream education and his stated career aspiration was 'when I leave school I want to be a painter and decorator'.

Service provider

Sunderland YOS, which is a partner of the South of Tyne ISSP Consortium.

Origins of the project and funding

The project was developed in 2005 to provide constructive work to supplement the education, training and employment requirements of an ISSP. Staff decided to provide a decorating project that gave training, a skills base and placements for the young people on the ISSP.

The costs of the project are met from the ISSP budget. In addition to staff costs the project funded an initial four-day plastering course for the project co-ordinator. The ongoing costs of materials are met by the YOS or the community projects that are being decorated.

Target group

The New Direction Project works with young people sentenced to an ISSP either as a sentence in its own right or as part of their licence conditions following release from custody. Most will spend six months on the ISSP.

This project targets young people on an ISSP who have no education, training or employment in place and who are outside statutory educational requirements, such as pupil referral units or in part-time education and training as part of an alternative to mainstream education.

What does the programme do?

The aim of the New Direction Project is to teach high tariff young offenders (active repeat young offenders and those who commit the most serious crimes) the skills of painting, decorating and plastering to help them secure future employment or training placements, which could help reduce the risk of future offending.

The first task of project staff is to break down barriers with the young people, such as developing trust with adults and interpersonal skills. This is achieved using hands-on construction activities like painting and decorating. They then progress onto work to challenge offending behaviour.

The New Direction Project identifies small-scale decoration projects as the focus for its work, like community centres. These projects are identified through the YOS Community Payback (see glossary) scheme and other local contacts. The community groups accept that projects may take longer to complete as the young people only work four hours per day but this is balanced by the negligible cost of the work. Working on small-scale projects enables the project co-ordinator to work closely and intensively with no more than two young people at a time. Young people develop their literacy and numeracy skills in tandem with the practical decorating skills. Their skills may also provide a springboard into future employment.

Client protocol and numbers

Each project is undertaken using two young people. A project co-ordinator will work with no more than three or four young people in a week on a community project. Young people will each work for approximately ten hours and can take between one and six months to complete a community project. In the past year the project has worked with 15 young people.

The project co-ordinator is flexible in his approach to working with the young people. He often supports them by ensuring they can get to placements.

To date no young person has breached their order. Staff on the project suggest that this is due to their close working relationships with the young people.

Staffing

The project co-ordinator works alone, although a substitute co-ordinator has been identified in case of absence. A case manager acts as the co-ordinator's line manager, who ensures that work on the project complements other work with the young person on the ISSP. Overall oversight rests with the ISSP manager.

Benefits of the scheme

The project provides the local community with high-quality decoration work, while the young people benefit from being taught skills which will help them to secure employment. The project has also been successful in attracting local press publicity that challenges public perceptions of young offenders within the community.

Monitoring, evaluation and effectiveness

The project is still in its infancy and has limited data upon which to assess its effectiveness. The project has been sent many letters of appreciation from grateful community projects which provide evidence of the value of the scheme. One such letter comes from Sunderland North Family Zone community project:

I am writing to you to let you know how our organization appreciated all the valuable help we received from the team. We took over the Hylton Castle Library in July last year and the whole building needed a makeover so if not for Andy and his team our building would still need a lot of work done to it. Andy and his team came along and really grafted and never complained; they were a pleasure to work with. I know in future that if we need any more work done or anything else for that matter, I would not hesitate to contact you again. So from the bottom of out hearts

A BIG THANK YOU FOR ALL YOUR SUPPORT.

Yours sincerely,

Eileen Cassley, Project Worker

Contact details:

Jim Sexton
ISSP Manager, A New Direction Project
Sunderland Youth Offending Team
Lambton House
145 High Street West
Sunderland
SR1 1UW

Tel: 0191 566 3000

Email: jim.sexton@sunderland.gov.uk

White Gold Project (WGP), Cornwall Youth Offending Team (CYOT)

Outstanding scheme award 2006

A client's experience

'Kevin' was a 16-year-old boy. He had lived in many places ranging from flats, bed-sits and foster care. In a 12-month period, the police linked 30 crimes to him including criminal damage, arson, ABH and threats to kill. He had been arrested 11 times.

WGP had made him an initial offer of support. He refused. However, a few months later he approached WGP asking for help. He had been thrown out of his family home. Problems had arisen around his father's alcoholism. WGP took him to the council homelessness department but found it difficult to place him, as an arson offence showed on his records. He had also technically made himself intentionally homeless. WGP negotiated a short-term solution with his father, who agreed to take him back.

As the police were already dealing with offences, Kevin was at risk of a custodial sentence. WGP supported him and provided information to the court about his efforts to improve his behaviour. Kevin was consequently sentenced to an ISSP, which was delivered by Cornwall Youth Offending Service.

Kevin left his family home. WGP helped find him temporary rented accommodation. He has stayed out of trouble although there are some issues with his alcohol and drug use. He has also secured full-time employment and accommodation for the past 12 months.

Service provider

WGP operates as part of the Cornwall YOT (see glossary). It is a partnership project between Devon and Cornwall Police, Cornwall County Safety Partnership and CYOT.

Origins of the programme and funding

WGP emerged from discussions between YOT and police managers. It started as a three-month pilot project in January 2003 in St Austell. It was managed by one police constable on secondment and was funded by the Crime and Disorder Partnership Group in Restormel. It initially targeted 12 known high-volume persistent young offenders with the aim of reducing youth crime.

WGP's initial success meant that it could secure funding which allowed more staff to be employed. It has also allowed it to extend the geographical coverage of the programme in Caradon, Carrick, North Cornwall, Restormel, Kerrier and Penwith districts of Cornwall.

The Devon and Cornwall Police basic command unit funds two police staff posts. A further two posts were created by the local public service agreement. The administrative support is seconded from the YOT.

Target group

Young people aged 10 to 19 years who are either already offending, or identified by the police as at risk of offending, work with WGP on a voluntary basis. Young people identified by the police as prolific offenders are proactively approached to take part.

WGP has devised an assessment tool that considers criminal risk factors and welfare issues to identify and target those young people who are most at risk, either through their current offending behaviour or at risk of becoming offenders. This assessment process produces two scores, one that indicates vulnerability and another that indicates potential criminality. If a young person has a combined score above 35% they are considered to be a good candidate for WGP intervention. Where a score between 30% and 35% is generated, the WGP will reassess the young person's needs to see if WGP should work with them. A score below 30% would lead to a referral to the YOT or other agencies as appropriate.

What does the programme do?

The aim of the WGP is to reduce youth crime by:

- producing quality assessments and information as a basis from which to address youth offending;
- ensuring high-quality partnership work to support positive changes by the young people; and
- ensuring high-quality partnership work to support and protect the community in the future.

The ethos of WGP is to offer persistent young offenders 'carrot and stick' options. WGP provides one-to-one support and co-ordinated help from a number of agencies in return for a change in behaviour. If young people fail to accept or comply with interventions it may lead to that young person becoming the focus of police targeting to hold them accountable for any anti-social or offending behaviour.

The daily work of the WGP workers is complex providing a mix of practical support and interventions to enable change. Interventions are tailored to the needs of the young person. WGP's ethos is that changes in a young person's lifestyle, family, behaviour, education and employment allow pathways away from offending to emerge. WGP staff work young people to address patterns of offending, self-esteem, confidence, anger issues, housing, education, mediation, personal responsibility, community impact, victim awareness, restorative justice, leisure interests, child protection issues, sexually inappropriate behaviour, drug issues, personal welfare and safety, family support and direct mobile links to other agencies.

Staff bring their own style of working with clients. They will support some by actually taking them to school while others will focus on finding a placement for the youngster. They encourage young people to access facilities within the community to keep them occupied and tap into new interests. One example is Tunnel Art in Newquay. This scheme works with young people on reparation orders following criminal damage convictions. The project produces positive and creative street art, using stencils, bold images and text. It uses art as a vehicle to create a positive environmental change and reduce criminal damage to the surrounding area. Young people are encouraged to maintain the area in partnership with local support agencies. Young people are given the opportunity to work towards the nationally recognised Art's Award qualification, which can lead to further education opportunities.

Client visit protocol

Once the WGP has identified a young person for intervention, a WGP worker will meet them. Initial visits are often 'cold calls'. They are used to provide information to the young person about the project and seek their agreement to participate. The young person will then sign a consent form which allows information to be exchanged across a range of agencies, for example, the police, health and social services.

Visits are usually at the young person's home but can also be in a mutually agreed location. Meetings are usually on a one-to-one basis after the initial visits. WGP operates a system of contact whereby staff assess each situation in terms of risk to the worker. If it is determined that a young person represents a high risk then staff will be accompanied by a manager or co-support worker.

Client numbers in the last year

The caseload of each member of staff varies from 15 to 25.

Monitoring

WGP has a strong recording and reporting system. As the project is linked to the police information system it uses this system to monitor the outcome of the WGP interventions. The WGP team assesses whether a young person has changed their behaviour based on whether they appear on the police intelligence system. This is regarded as evidence that they are succeeding in changing attitudes and behaviour in the short term. If the young person remains clear of the police intelligence system, success is regarded as being longer term.

Staffing

Devon and Cornwall Police employ all WGP staff. This means they can use police information and IT systems. The staff team includes seven full-time staff and a part-time administrator. There is one project manager and six outreach support workers.

The project manager is responsible for the day-to-day management. Weekly team briefings are used to discuss any issues arising and the caseload. Monthly team meetings are used to provide input from partner agencies and staff training.

The project manager is line managed by the Cornwall YOT manager. In addition, WGP has a steering group which oversees its development and monitors its progress in terms of finance, recruitment and client outcomes, ensures compliance to other agencies' processes and procedures, and ensures effective, efficient service delivery. The steering group draws members from: the community safety officer group; the Devon and Cornwall Police basic command unit; the Cornwall YOT manager, the WGP project manager; and the county community safety sergeant. The steering group meets quarterly.

Benefits

Feedback from family members and service users have been very positive about the programme. The following testimonies from those individuals involved with WGP highlight the benefits, and the level of dedication and hard work from WGP staff (Barton and Teagle 2004):

He's had a very positive effect on my son and his outlook on life as well. You can definitely see a change in his attitudes when he's come back from a [WGP] session. My son's built up a strong relationship with ****, he shares things with him. He's the only person who's been of any help to my son.

Parent of a service user

I was all over the place I didn't know where to turn. So I think [WGP] was a turning point, no hesitation in saying that, absolutely.

Service user

If you contact them its action, with social services it's like 'sure we'll do that, and we'll do this' and it doesn't get done until a week or two later. As small as that sounds it really is a big difference.

Service user

Evaluation and effectiveness

The University of Plymouth (Barton and Teagle 2004) evaluated the WGP in 2004. The research indicated that:

- since 2003 the project had used existing police intelligence to focus on 400 young people (78% male and 22% female);
- of the 400, WGP worked with 169 young people, monitoring the remaining 230 using the police intelligence system for signs of increased risk and the need for intervention; and
- the average number of crimes linked to the young person pre-WGP intervention was 4.3. The number fell to 1.8 crimes post-intervention.

The evaluation concluded that WGP had worked with an impressive number of clients. Even given caveats about evaluating social crime prevention interventions and the reliance on qualitative data to measure outcomes, it found that WGP had a positive impact on the levels of youth crime with an accompanying cost saving and positive impact on the life in local communities. Finally, the research noted the increased levels of police intelligence that was gathered as a result of the WGP.

Contact details:

Alan Milliner
White Gold Project Manager, Cornwall YOT
Chiltern House
City Road
Truro
Cornwall
TR1 2JL
Tel: 01872 274567
Email: amilliner@cornwall.gov.uk

IMPACT – Inclusive Model of Partnership Against Car Theft, Belfast

Scheme of special merit 2005

Service provider and origins of the programme

Car crime has been a significant community issue in Greater West Belfast for many years. The Probation Board for Northern Ireland (PBNI) had supported many projects over the past 20 years to try to tackle the issue.

IMPACT started in October 2001. It employs a partnership model that is built upon two fundamental premises. First, the initiative adopts as inclusive an approach as possible and second, that the operational staff team would need to be drawn from a range of backgrounds to reflect the partner agencies.

There are several key stakeholders including the PBNI, the police and the youth justice agency. Political sensitivities in West Belfast created difficulties in relation to the role that the Police Service of Northern Ireland (PSNI) could play. Some sections of the community refused to attend meetings with the police. Therefore it was agreed that an advisory panel, consisting of the PSNI and other statutory agencies would convene to advise on the role and scope of the project. A steering committee was also established to help manage the project. Its membership was drawn equally from the local community and the statutory partners.

Funding

The Northern Ireland Office (NIO) has provided around £387k for the project to support the work since its inception in 2001 (£250K for the first three years and £137k in the financial year 2004/05). A further two years' funding was then allocated until March 2008.

In addition, several of the partner agencies seconded staff to the project team.

Target group

The group work programmes target 10- to 17-year-olds who are serious and/or persistent offenders with current or previous histories of car crime offences. IMPACT works with young people in prison, either under sentence or on remand, as long as there is time to complete the course. The project provides support for parents of the young people referred onto the programme.

What does the programme do?

IMPACT is a joint community-statutory response to the issue of car crime. Its main aim is to work in partnership and build solutions that will help reduce and prevent car theft within a geographical area. Two broad themes inform the work: awareness and empathy for victims; and the consequences of actions for both those involved in car crime and for the wider community.

The project works in a range of environments including prisons, youth centres, probation offices, primary and secondary schools, community-based premises and sometimes street locations.

IMPACT has adopted a strategic approach to tackling the issue of car crime on three levels:

Level 1: Intervention work with those who are actively engaged in car crime offences.

The project uses both individual and group work in a range of settings for sentenced prisoners, those serving community sentences and on a voluntary basis.

The scheme delivers the ten-session 'Your Choice' car crime programme to groups of up to eight people. Two members of staff deliver the two-hour sessions twice a week for five weeks. It aims to challenge offending behaviour and encourage individuals to take responsibility for their life and choices. Each participant's offending is examined to identify risk factors and strategies for avoiding offending behaviour in the future. Issues covered in the sessions include:

- attitudes, beliefs and opinions in relation to car crime;
- discussions about community objections to car crime and to look at their cognitive distortions that might predicate their engagement in car crime;
- thinking straight and awareness raising session, looking at why they steal cars, what makes it difficult for them to think 'straight' and reasons for their offending behaviour;
- victim awareness and the effects of car crime on the rest of the community and the young person's consequential thinking. The session uses video sequences showing the damage to lives due to stolen cars, accidents and deaths; and
- the last group session looks at 'staying out of cars', focusing on what led individuals to get into stolen cars; what type of things they did before they started getting into cars and kept out of trouble; and what can help them stay away from stolen cars in the future. The session looks at exploring alternative strategies and avoidance techniques to stay out of trouble.

Level 2: Diversionary work with those on the margins of this behaviour.

This work often focuses on groups of young people who act as an audience for those driving stolen cars. It is often derived from requests from local communities who help identify and pinpoint a problem group. To support this strand of IMPACT's work, multi-agency partnerships (including West Belfast Area Project, Training for Life, Terry Enright Foundation) have been established. This intervention project was set up as a direct response to ongoing anti-social behaviour in the Upper Springfield area of Belfast. The main focus of this work is a Friday and Saturday night 'drop in' facility providing young people the opportunity to engage in informal group work on a range of issues, including bullying, sexual health, community relations, anger management, peer pressure, conflict resolution and healthy living. These issues are facilitated through the medium of sport, the arts, on the streets by detached workers and through structured group work.

Level 3: Preventative work with young people who are vulnerable to involvement in such behaviour.

This work targets the sub-culture that supports, and perpetrates, car theft. Car crime awareness education programmes are delivered in local schools, youth projects and via outreach work to help young people address the attitudes, beliefs and myths that are used to rationalise anti-social activity. It can be delivered to primary and secondary school children in an education and prevention programme. There are four sessions looking at the impact of car crime, discussing the effects of car crime on the community, family and friends by using discussions, scenario sessions and videos.

Client numbers in the last year

Intervention work

Between August 2006 and 30 September 2007, 113 people were referred to IMPACT for intervention work. This included 60 adults (20 statutory and 40 voluntary referrals) and 53 children (30 statutory and 23 voluntary referrals).

During the same period, two parent support groups took place. Each group was made up of parents of young people who were involved in car crime and lasted for ten weeks. The first group had a core attendance of five parents, while the second group had four.

There were four 'Your Choice' programmes delivered in Hydebank Young Offenders' Centre. Of the 29 who started the programme, 22 completed. A further 30 young people, aged between 13 and 17 years, completed the four-session programme at the Woodland Juvenile Justice Centre.

Prevention work

In the year to September 2007, 618 young people received the education and prevention programme in nine schools (three secondary schools and six primary schools)

During the summer months a number of sessions were delivered to 104 6-to 17-year-olds. With younger children the sessions incorporated making posters and T-shirt painting, whilst information sessions were used for older children.

Monitoring

Many tools are used to monitor the progress and effectiveness of the programmes delivered by the scheme, including:

- pre-group and post-group interviews, motivation and attitude assessments;
- group session feedback forms;
- teacher evaluation forms; and
- end of programme evaluation forms completed by clients and facilitators.

Pre-course attitudinal questionnaire for young people in years 8 – 10

1. A group of friends are watching stolen cars, would you watch with them?

Circle one number only

Yes	1	Go to question 2
No	2	Go to question 3

2. If you think you would watch stolen cares with friends what would the things be that you would like about it?

Circle ANY that you agree with

The fun/excitement	1
The speed	2
Being with the group	3
Something to do	4
Cheering people I know	5
Something else. Please write what that would be.	6

3. A group of friends have stolen a car and they have asked you to go along with them for a ride. Would you:

Circle one number only

Say no	1
Go along with them but not be happy about it	2
Go along with them and enjoy it	3

4. Imagine that you were involved with stealing a car. Do you think you would enjoy it?

Circle one number only

Yes	1	Go to question 5
No	2	Go to question 6

5. If you think you would enjoy it, what do you think would be the things that you would like about stealing a car?

Circle ANY that you agree with

The excitement of stealing	1
The speed	2
Avoiding the police	3
Being with your friends	4
The challenge of starting the car	5
Something else. Please write what that would be.	6

6. Imagine that you were involved with stealing a car. Do you think you would worry about it?

Circle one number only

Yes	1	Go to question 7
No	2	Go to question 8

7. If you worry about it, what would you worry about?

Circle ANY that you agree with

Being punished by your parents	1
Being caught by the police	2
Being punished by others	3
Crashing and hurting myself	4
Injuring one of my friends	5
Injuring someone else	6
Something else. Please write what that would be.	7

8. Imagine that you were driving a stolen car. Do you think you would worry about it?

Circle one number only

Yes	1	Go to question 9
No	2	Go to question 10

9. If you worry about it, what would you worry about?

Circle ANY that you agree with

Being punished by your parents	1
Being caught by the police	2
Being punished by others	3
Crashing and hurting myself	4
Injuring one of my friends	5
Injuring someone else	6
Something else. Please write what that would be.	7

10. Imagine that you were a passenger in a stolen car; do you think you would worry about it?

Circle one number only

Yes	1	Go to question 11
No	2	

11. If you would worry about it, what would you worry about?

Circle ANY that you agree with

Being punished by your parents	1
Being caught by the police	2
Being punished by others	3
Crashing and hurting myself	4
Injuring one of my friends	5
Injuring someone else	6
Something else. Please write what that would be.	7

Thank you for completing this questionnaire.

The scheme uses team meetings as practice development sessions where they share ideas, monitoring the progress of cases and sharing skills.

An example of IMPACT's monitoring process can be highlighted for the Intervention Project where:

- each session is followed by staff evaluation and a report completed outlining both statistical and qualitative information;
- the following forms are completed for bi-weekly meetings – session plans, group evaluation forms, time sheets and outreach/detached recording sheets;

- each group work session enables young people to help plan and evaluate their participation in projects; this will be either orally, in writing or in photo format; and

- copies of all notes, minutes, photos, consent forms etc. are retained as evidence and are presented to those parties and organisations involved in the financing, planning and management of the projects.

Staffing

The project structures are:

- steering committee (16 organisations contribute including statutory, community, voluntary and political sectors, including Belfast Education Library Board, Youth Justice Agency, Glen Parent Support Group, PBNI);

- advisory panel (six organisations contribute to the advisory panel including the NIO, PSNI, NIACRO, North and West Belfast HSST, PBNI and Down Lisburn HSST.[2] Here, the membership spans statutory and voluntary sectors);

- operational manager's liaison contacts (two staff from PSNI);

- IMPACT operational staff team (five individuals); and

- mentors (three locally-based volunteers).

The IMPACT team staff structure includes: one operational manager; one senior practitioner (part-time), seconded from Youth Justice Agency; two probation service officers, seconded from NIO and PBNI; and one administrator.

---

2   This is part of the leaving and after-care services.

Benefits of the scheme

There is strong evidence that IMPACT has positively changed the attitudes and behaviour of the young people who engage with the project. Research and Evaluation Services (2004) carried out a telephone survey of IMPACT's clients and stakeholders and found that:

- 94% thought that IMPACT's work would help them to avoid getting involved in car crime in the future;
- 97% had become more aware of the consequences of crime; and
- 97% thought more about victims.

Parents and carers of the young people who have worked with IMPACT have reported it to be a great comfort and support. They felt that the project prevented their child from getting involved in car crime and that they received good practical advice from project staff. In relation to the community, the main benefits that have been reported are:

- a feeling of being heard and supported;
- that the project was a safe place to seek support; and
- an acknowledgement that statutory agencies, including those from the criminal justice sector, could be involved without the project becoming unacceptable locally.

There has been a reduction in car crime in West Belfast since the start of the project, and car crime has fallen by more than the 10% target set by the NIO:

- the level of unauthorised takings of cars has fallen by 92%;
- the level of recovered vehicles is down by 47%;
- the level of vehicle theft has gone down by 22%; and
- the level of vehicle tampering has declined by 19%.

Evaluation and effectiveness

The project has been conducting and documenting internal, formal evaluations for the programmes they have delivered. The project has also developed a psychometric tool to measure attitudinal shifts in the young people who engage with them. Research and Evaluation Services (RES) conducted an independent evaluation of the work of the project, with the first period of evaluation taking place between 2001 and 2004 (Research and Evaluation Services 2004) and with a final report also produced for the period April 2004 to March 2005 (Research and Evaluation Services 2005). Results from 2005 showed that:

- those who had been involved in the IMPACT programme had committed significantly fewer and less serious offences one year post-engagement; this suggested a real reduction in car crime and not displacement;
- overall, almost three-quarters (30 cases) of the participants examined were not convicted of any car crime offences in the 12-month period after the completion of their IMPACT programme;
- less than 25% (ten out of 43) were convicted a year after receiving IMPACT interventions and even in these cases the gravity and frequency of their involvement in car crime was significantly reduced; and
- in all, 93% of the participants examined had made a positive change in their car crime behaviour post-completion (that is, either no further convictions were recorded or the gravity and severity of convictions was reduced).

Contact details:

IMPACT
Sally Gardens Community Centre
Bell Street Road
Poleglass
Belfast
BT17 0PB

Tel: 02890627321

Email: admin@theimpactproject.org.uk

CHAPTER 6

Education, Training, Employment and Mentoring

Not having a job is one of the major factors associated with reoffending. There is a strong correlation between offending and poor literacy, language and numeracy skills, low achievement and school truancy as well as low self-esteem. Many people who offend have a poor experience of education and little stable employment (The Howard League for Penal Reform 2006). A lack of recent work experience will compound these barriers for many ex-offenders, and employer discrimination is often reported. There are also issues about how to constructively disclose a criminal record to potential employers (Fletcher, Woodhill and Herrington 1998).

The Howard League for Penal Reform's Community Programmes Award winners have demonstrated the value of providing their clients with structured learning plans and guidance to aid their progress into future education, training and employment. Fletcher, Woodhill and Herrington (1998) identified ten good practice issues when working with this client group including networking and local co-ordination; developing trust and motivation; assessing; action planning and reviewing; disclosure; and monitoring and evaluation. Our award winners engage in many of these practices. In particular, networking and local community co-ordination has helped many of the project's service users gain employment and training. The Access Team, for example, provides a clear example of how working closely with employers, agencies and educational establishments enables them to provide clients with effective advice and support.

Warbarth, The Access Team and Resettlement and Aftercare Provision (RAP), all use mentors to help to establish trust and build motivation amongst their service users, which, in turn, encourages them to find training and employment. All the projects work with their clients in their own communities on an outreach basis if necessary. Mentors work closely with service users on a one-to-one basis based on individualised action plans. The ability to focus on individual need is paramount.

Warbarth Project, Working Links and Devon and Cornwall Probation Area (DCPA)

Outstanding scheme award 2007

A client's experience

'Roger' was advised to find out more about Warbarth by his probation officer and an appointment was made the following day. At the first meeting with his Warbarth adviser, he identified some issues with confidence and his concerns about having to go through an interview in order to get the job he wanted as a chef. Time was spent with Roger on his interview skills as well as helping with some suitable clothes for interviews. When he was feeling ready Warbarth helped him start his job search.

Roger had severe diabetes and this meant his vision was affected and he was not medically fit to drive. Warbarth provided bus passes for him whilst he was looking for a job and for his first few months in work.

In the past Roger had committed several burglaries so Warbarth advised him to consider offering to do work trials to show prospective employers his skills. With his adviser's help he approached local pubs and restaurants and eventually a trial was forthcoming. Warbarth provided Roger with his chef's whites.

After completing his trial Roger talked to his adviser about disclosing his conviction. They approached the employer for a three-way meeting. Roger had worked hard, and because of the support he was getting, his employer wanted to give Roger a chance. He started his new job the next day.

Roger enjoyed his work and felt that he had a brighter future. His confidence and self-esteem were boosted and he felt he had his independence back.

Service provider

This is a partnership project between Working Links and the lead contractor, Devon and Cornwall Probation Area (DCPA). Working Links is a public/private/ voluntary partnership set up to help people who are long-term unemployed, find work. Through its work with the probation service, Warbarth (meaning togetherness in Cornish) brings together two different sets of expertise.

Origins of the programme

The project was formed in May 2006 as a joint venture to facilitate access to education, training and employment. It was a response to the UK's National Action Plan to Reduce Reoffending (Department of Justice 2004), which reported that 75% of prisoners leave prison with no paid employment and that 55% of those on community sentences are unemployed at the start of their orders. Fifty-two per cent of males and 71% of females start their sentences with no qualifications.

The National Action Plan also identified a poor uptake of education by offenders after release from prison. It noted a key factor to be the incompatibility between education provision in prison and the community. It also noted a mismatch between the course start dates and prisoners' release dates and a reluctance to employ or accept people with a criminal record on courses. Warbarth was launched as a means to help alleviate some of these issues.

Funding

Warbarth is a joint venture between Working Links and DCPA. It is overseen by the Warbarth Project Management Group, and financed through the European Social Fund's (ESF) (see glossary) Objective One funding, with matched funding from DCPA and Working Links. Funding is secured until June 2008.

Target group

Warbarth works with people who are subject to statutory supervision by the probation service or returning to Cornwall after release from short prison sentences. They must be unemployed and over 18 years old.

Referrals

Potential clients have to seek out the service. However clients tend to be directed to Warbarth via three routes:

- non-statutory referrals: this can be a self-referral through Jobcentre Plus or by other community and voluntary sector groups;
- probation supervision: these referrals are made by probation officers; and
- referrals by a prison.

Over 50% of referrals come via the DCPA, with other organisations such as Jobcentre Plus providing a significant number of referrals.

Once a referral is accepted, the performance manager considers the client's probation service client risk assessment, which includes relevant information on topics such as multi-agency public protection arrangements (MAPPA) (see glossary). The quality and finance administrator then processes the referrals and allocates them to a Warbarth consultant within 24 hours. The consultant reviews the individual's risk assessment, case history (where available), and any conditions that they may be obliged to comply with (for example, statutory curfews) before setting up an initial consultation with the client. This can take up to a week.

What does the programme do?

Warbarth is sub-contracted by DCPA to provide individuals with holistic, bespoke packages of support. This includes practical help to access employment, training or education programmes and ongoing support in the first three months of starting a placement or job. There is no 'off the shelf' package, as clients work with an adviser to address their own personal barriers. The programme is voluntary and free. Clients dictate the frequency and kind of service they receive.

A client and their adviser will work through various issues including:

- CV writing, interview practice and techniques;
- opening a bank account;
- providing help to pay for practical things like transport, tools and clothing (see below);
- finding accommodation;
- marketing clients to employers;
- criminal disclosure workshops; and
- accessing training or education.

During the initial consultation the adviser and client explore issues that might be barriers to work, and their current skills and qualifications. This will lead to a bespoke support package and action plan being developed. The action plan identifies the support that will be given to help them pursue realistic and sustainable employment, education or training. Both the client and the adviser sign this action plan.

Advisers all work on an outreach basis and are flexible in their approach to delivery. They use libraries, cafés, supermarkets, local community centres, sports centres,

Jobcentre Plus offices and probation offices to meet people in their own community.

Wherever possible the client will see the same personal adviser. Each adviser has an average caseload of around 50, and sees each client as often as they both feel is necessary, but usually this is at least once per fortnight. Each adviser spends approximately 20 hours per week with different clients. The length of time that Warbarth staff work with an individual is determined by their level of need, which is largely client driven.

Warbarth clients have access to a £500 (maximum) subsidy (the Warbarth *'client pot'*) that can be spent on anything they need to facilitate their ability to obtain (and sustain) employment, training or education. This is allocated on a needs-led basis according to specific guidelines and can be spent at any stage of a client's progress. For example, funding has been made available for such things as: driving lessons to help overcome the travel problems in rural locations within the county; forklift driver training; horticultural and construction courses; as well as first aid and health and safety awareness training.

Support is provided for three months after an individual has been successfully placed in sustainable employment or training.

Client numbers and performance

Between July 2006 and March 2007, Warbarth had worked with 349 clients with the following outcomes:

- 80 clients found suitable employment;
- 17 have sustained their employment;
- 58 have started training;
- 33 accessed further education; and
- 29 received qualifications.

Staffing

The Warbarth team includes:

- one performance manager who oversees delivery of the project and supervises consultants;
- four personal consultants who work on an individual basis with clients;
- one quality and finance administrator who ensures contract compliance and provides general administrative support; and
- one part-time delivery manager who provides supervision, support and guidance for the performance manager, as well as work on new business development.

Monitoring

Consultants have regular caseload reviews with their manager. They also work in partnership with probation officers to ensure that a realistic plan is being delivered. There is a high level of collaboration between individual advisers who regularly share their knowledge and expertise to ensure that clients get the best support and advice.

Through Working Links the project has access to management information systems which measure their performance against the targets set for the project. They also produce a monthly return for the European Social Fund and DCPA.

Benefits of the scheme

Warbarth negotiates with prospective employers to help clients gain employment. It also provides support and advice in setting up their own businesses. Six people have achieved this so far. In one instance, two clients – a photographer and an artist – were put in contact with each other to form a successful business. Both had started test trading through New Deal (see glossary) for self-employment. Their Working Links adviser had arranged free business support from Truro College. The Warbarth adviser soon realised that both these new businesses could start helping each other. The photographer was having problems with framing, and the artist was skilled at framing but didn't have the equipment. By helping to purchase some framing tools, both businesses are now working together.

Warbarth has established excellent relationships within the area. For example, it has joined forces with Jobcentre Plus, Cornwall Works and Plymouth Argyle (football club) in the community. The two-week activity programme, Kick Off, works with young offenders in deprived areas. Participants complete the Level 1 Football Association coaching certificate and attend sessions on healthy eating, teamwork and motivation and basic skills provision. Excellent collaborations have also been made with local employers, for example Jamie Oliver's Fifteen restaurant, which directly employed a client.

Evaluation

The University of Plymouth evaluated Warbarth in August 2007 (Southern *et al.* 2007). It found that the project had reached more than double its original targets for client contact. It also found that:

- 32 out of the 50 clients in the sample group, said they were happy with their referral;
- the majority of respondents said that being referred made them feel good and supported;
- 70% of the respondents felt their expectations of the service had been fully met, for example, many had reservations due to barriers around access to

employment, self-esteem, and the stigma of having a criminal record, but the scheme had helped them overcome these issues;

- 34% of the respondents stated that they had received financial support to help them with a variety of needs – purchase clothes for work, take driving tests;
- Warbarth was able to provide continued support after individuals were placed in employment, education or training which helped people move beyond the short-lived employment into sustainable employment;
- the project's success was based on the effective communication and collaboration between DCPA and Warbarth staff, in particular, sharing information;
- 84% of respondents stated the level of support they received was very good; clients particularly highlighted the one-to-one support, assistance with CV writing; the immediacy of Warbarth's response to requests for support; and targeted support with addressing basic needs such as food and shelter; and
- 86% were happy with, and satisfied with, the project.

Contact details:

Zena Gardener
Performance Manager, Warbarth, Working Links
7 Lower Bore Street, Bodmin,
Cornwall, PL31 2JR

Tel: 01208 79951

Email: zena.gardner@workinglinks.co.uk

Access Team, Nottinghamshire Probation Area

Scheme of special merit award 2007

A client's experience

'Richard' was offered employment with a local construction firm following the support of the Access Team.

At the age of 14 years he had dropped out of the education system and now, aged 32 years, had an entrenched history of offending to fund a serious heroin addiction.

While under the supervision of Nottinghamshire Probation Area he was encouraged to seek the support of the Access Team. Richard attended disclosure and job-seeking workshops, IT training and in-house basic skills provision through which he achieved an OCR[3] in numeracy.

The team enabled him to access funding to take CCS (Construction Certification Scheme) (see glossary) and a health and safety test. He was supported to apply for an ECTA (Nottingham Environmental Construction Training for All) course in groundwork with employed status. He was nervous at the prospect of starting training, so to allay his fears, the team arranged an accompanied visit to his place of work before starting the programme. The team's benefit advisor carried out an 'in works benefit calculation' to optimise his income.

Richard completed his six-months' construction training and gained his NVQ Level 1 in groundwork. He also achieved certificates in manual handling, first aid, abrasive wheels and working at heights.

Richard worked with the company for a while, although he eventually

---

3   OCR (Oxford Cambridge and RSA Examinations) is a leading UK awarding body, committed to providing qualifications that engage learners of all ages at school, college, in work or through part-time learning programmes to achieve their full potential. It offers a wide range of general and vocational qualifications that equip learners with the knowledge and skills they need for their future.

*moved on to a different construction company. He carried on to enjoy his
new job and lifestyle. He was keeping fit, healthy and drug free for the
first time in his adult life and this was his longest period of time without
offending.*

Service provider

The Access Team is Nottinghamshire Probation Area's
resource for unemployed offenders. The service forms
an integral part of community supervision and offender
management.

Origins of the programme

Nottinghamshire Probation Area recognised that
barriers to work and training had been created by a lack
of understanding of the Rehabilitation of Offenders
Act 1974 (see glossary). To overcome this, it created the
role of employer engagement officer, within the Access
Team, to work with employers, agencies and educational
establishments to advise, educate and support them in
every aspect of offender education, recruitment and
employment.

Funding

The probation team has been running employment
projects for offenders since 1976. The Access Team has
been in existence since April 1999.

The Access Team is funded from mainstream and
partnership sources, for example, Neighbourhood Renewal
Fund (see glossary) and Connexions. (see glossary) The
team has also been very successful in securing grants from
the county council for activities, which reduce the barriers
individual offenders face in getting into work, such as drug
or alcohol misuse. Team funding is regularly reviewed and
the potential to be more cost-effective is always explored.

The team has moved premises and a secondment to another related organisation has been arranged.

Target group

People who are sentenced to a community order (see glossary) or on licence from prison are eligible for support. Clients must be unemployed, on incapacity benefit, or a lone parent.

What does the programme do?

Support from the Access Team forms part of the end-to-end management process and aims to meet the needs of an offender's supervision plan. Attendance on the programme is built into their supervision plan, therefore missed appointments can result in breaching their order.

Employment officers within the Access Team work with clients to identify any barriers to employment, training and education, including a lack of qualifications, problems with confidence and self-esteem, or issues surrounding the disclosure of their previous offences. They offer practical help and realistic advice to improve clients' employability, and assist them in finding and keeping employment. Core service interventions include: information, advice and guidance sessions; disclosure of offences; CV building; job seeking; employer engagement; and skills for life. The work with clients is initially on a one-to-one basis. It is based on individual client need and the resultant action plan. The Access Team adapts its working methods to incorporate the needs of a range of individuals from different circumstances and cultural backgrounds. As the work with the client develops, group work can be introduced.

Staff work closely with local and community projects to support their work and gain optimum benefit for the client. The team places a high priority on public protection considerations. This is supported by ensuring that there is a close working relationship with partner organisations and relevant information sharing.

Examples of opportunities that have been found for clients include:

- Unique projects bridging gaps in statutory provision by enabling access to short commercial training courses such as site licences and contractor's safety passports. Courses can be booked at very short notice and enable the team to react to changes in the local job market extremely efficiently.

- A partnership with an agency that recruits for local power stations. The agency contacts the team when a contract is imminent, which enables motivated offenders to apply for vacancies. Project money enables each offender to do their Client Contractor's National Safety Guild card, which is required to access power station sites.

- A project which motivates service users to drive legally, through gaining provisional licences, theory tests and compulsory basic training tests not only provides a form of identification but also a means of travelling to their place of work, essential in rural areas.

The Access Team's employer engagement officer works with employers, agencies and educational establishments to advise, educate, train and support them in every aspect of offender education, recruitment and employment and to assist them in using the Rehabilitation of Offenders Act as a tool to enable informed decision making.

Employers and agencies are approached to review their recruitment and employment policies, and develop and implement procedures that support the employer to allow offenders to apply and be recruited for appropriate jobs. The team continually receives feedback from service users who have been refused work at agencies, for example, as most do not accept applications from anyone with an unspent offence.

A business-to-business approach has been the key to opening the door with employers, building rapport and trust, marketing the benefits and support available.

Client numbers

Approximately 3,000 clients use the service each year. The Access Team works to targets set nationally, which measure the number of clients gaining employment, and remaining employed for four weeks. Monitoring data is submitted using the NPS database and fed back to the Home Office.

In the period April 2006 to the end of March 2007, a total of 566 Nottinghamshire offenders gained employment, of whom 395 retained their employment for four weeks or more.

Staffing

The team is composed of nine employment officers based around Nottingham. The team manager is based at the Nottinghamshire Probation Area headquarters. A research and data administrative assistant supports the team.

Recent success stories

- The Access Team approached several employment agencies and found that their clients had problems adhering to the guidelines of their professional body, the Recruitment and Employment Confederation (REC) (see glossary). In order to resolve the issue, a meeting was organised with the REC's external communications director. The Access Team managed to secure a commitment to address the problem. Over time, the team met with the REC's legal team and diversity forum and agreed a strategy for positive change to their guidelines. The REC consequently developed guidelines to recruit and employ offenders. Every member agency now receives supporting information in the bi-monthly legal and diversity communications. The REC has 7,000 corporate members and 5,000 individual members. These changes to guidelines allow offenders nationally an opportunity to be considered for many more jobs from which they would have been excluded.

- The Access Team secured an agreement from DHL at the B&Q national distribution centre to ensure applications that are directly referred by the team, are fairly considered and handled

- The Access Team has worked with local colleges and universities to develop a system to ensure they have access to relevant information on offenders applying to study. The team also delivers sessions to students, particularly those studying business, about employing people who have had convictions, on the basis that these are the employers of tomorrow.

Supporting People Fund (see glossary) to add support for accommodation, especially for those who are homeless or at risk of becoming homeless. Funding is guaranteed until March 2008. However, in a recent YJB review, funding has been provisionally extended for another year. The Supporting People money has been agreed until 2009.

Target group

RAP works mainly with young people on detention and training orders (DTOs) and those on community orders (see glossary) who are referred by a Drug Education Counselling and Confidential Advice (DECCA) or CAMHS (see glossary) worker who works within the SYOS. All young people referred onto the scheme must have a postal address in Sandwell.

What does the programme do?

The scheme resettles young people back into the community after:

- being in custody; or
- receiving a community order; and
- having substance misuse and/or mental health issues.

RAP is a voluntary programme aimed at young people in Sandwell who have substance misuse issues and/or mental health issues. The scheme provides assistance with accommodation, education, training and employment for young people for up to 25 hours per week. It also provides family support, life skills training and helps them find constructive leisure time pursuits.

This is achieved though intensive and confidential one-to-one support and mentoring. The scheme can work with young people for up to six months after their order has ended. After this period a drop-in service is available for support and/or guidance. The scheme has worked with young people for varying lengths of time, from three months to two years.

A mentor will build up a relationship with a young person, from custody through to release, or from the initial meeting they have with the young person. If the young person is in a custodial establishment a RAP worker will visit them on a regular basis. A resettlement plan is then written in consultation with the young person. The plan is broken down into nine sections of need or risk: accommodation arrangements; parents/carers; peer relationships; substance misuse and/or mental health issues; education; training or employment opportunities; use of leisure time; life and basic skills as well as any other areas the young person feels could stop them living a crime-free life. Once the initial resettlement plan is devised it is reviewed with the young person and all relevant agencies after the first week, and then on a monthly basis.

The young person generally meets with their mentor three or four times per week so that the plan can be reviewed on a daily basis if required. Mentors and clients meet as often as needed throughout the week, up to a maximum of 25 hours. This can include evening and weekend work.

The project's activities include:

- accredited college courses;
- music production;
- martial arts;
- beauty therapy;
- job search;
- education support;
- one-2-one mentoring; and
- life skills.

RAP mentors accompany young people to any identified activities for the initial visit but they may continue to accompany them if it is appropriate. If they do not have direct provision, the scheme is able to find new activities from ideas generated by the young person. All new providers are checked, risk assessed, and passed (if acceptable) as appropriate to work with the young people. Providers deliver a range of accredited programmes from nail art to fork lift truck driving. The young person decides on the activity they wish to engage in, which means the project is constantly sourcing new providers.

RAP works with a range of agencies to meet all needs of young people and offer ongoing one-to-one support throughout the term of their licence or order. All RAP interventions take place in the community, preferably within the young person's local area, to encourage the feeling of community involvement. Restorative principles are encouraged throughout RAP practices, which involves young people being aware of the consequences of their actions and the impact this may have on their community and on them as a member of that community.

RAP is voluntary, therefore a young person cannot be beached for missing appointments. However, if they do stop attending, RAP staff will attempt to bring them back onto the programme by identifying any difficulties and working with them to resolve those issues.

There are a number of ways in which contact is terminated:

- planned end as a negotiated process;
- young person decides to disengage; or
- young person persistently does not attend and staff are unable to establish contact.

Staff caseloads vary depending on individual client's need, so a worker may have ten low-level cases, or four high-level cases. The service aims to be flexible, but in general staff would have between three and six high-level cases and then a decision would be made as to how many further cases they could reasonably manage. The scheme allocates approximately 104 hours of staff time per week to the project. Sixty per cent of this is client contact, including face-to-face and telephone contact.

Client numbers

In the year ending June 2007, RAP worked with 59 clients.

Table 6.1. Number of clients by age, sex and diversity monitoring

Age	13 years	14 years	15 years	16 years	17 years
	1	14	10	16	18
Sex	Male	Female			
	46	13			
Diversity monitoring	White British	White Irish	Black British	Dual heritage	Asian
	47	1	5	4	2

Monitoring

A young person's plan is regularly reviewed and updated as necessary, and changes are implemented weekly. As young people have ownership of their programmes, and reviews are built into the process, most of the clients do participate. If they feel they want to disengage, then their mentor would encourage them to re-engage and address any issues, which may preclude them from participating.

Monitoring the effectiveness of work is an ongoing process. Young people complete evaluation forms on a monthly basis to feed back information to the team on the service provided.

A standing item on the team meeting agenda is case reviews. This provides an opportunity to share the progress of a young person and creates a forum to share good practice. In-house training for staff is regularly available, and the supervision process highlights the needs and gaps in provision to both staff and young people.

The RAP management team meets regularly to review staff tasks and workload.

All service level agreements are reviewed annually.

Staffing

The staff team is made up of a RAP project manager, team leader, and mentors. Three staff are full-time and one part-time. No staff have left RAP since its inception.

Evaluation and effectiveness

Only 18 young people have breached their order while working with RAP. RAP has no formal targets set by the YJB. However, when the initial bid was submitted to the YJB, it proposed to work with 30 young people and the aim was for 10% to successfully complete the programme. This baseline has been exceeded.

The SYOS has recently reviewed the project and involved team members, practitioners within the SYOS, and young people. This led the project to seek out more providers and improve progress records.

Contact details:

Kate Duffy
RAP (Resettlement & Aftercare Provision) Team Leader
Sandwell YOS
SGS House
Johns Lane
Tipton Road
Oldbury
B69 3HX

Tel: 0121 557 8804

Email: kate_duffy@sandwell.gov.uk

CHAPTER 7

Unpaid Work and Training

There are 12 different elements that can be combined by a sentencer in a community order (see glossary): one of them is unpaid work. This work must be for the benefit of the community. Unpaid work allows offenders to learn cognitive and practical skills while under intensive supervision. Unpaid work supervisors are trained to act as positive role models and to encourage the development of positive attitudes and behaviour towards work, other individuals and the wider community.

Forest Research's Offenders and Nature Scheme (O&N) involves clients working as volunteers on nature conservation and woodland sites. Alongside the work there are opportunities to address issues that may contribute to offending, like poor education. Qualifications are offered to enhance a client's future employability. Similarly, the Dorset Community Service Unit has developed a programme with the Tank Museum at Bovington Camp. Clients have been supported to achieve awards in literacy, numeracy, and develop engineering skills. The aim is to introduce 'valued added' skills to offenders sentenced to community sentences.

Offenders and Nature Schemes (O&N), Forestry Commission

Outstanding scheme award 2007

Since 2004, probationers from Tunbridge Wells and Tonbridge in Kent have carried out a wide range of tasks on Forestry Commission land to benefit the local community and visitors to Bedgebury Forest. Work parties consist of up to 25 people to carry out reparative work under the supervision of a probation officer. Each Sunday a large group of 18- to 25-year-olds worked on the schemes and two slightly smaller groups, generally aged 25 to 50 years, worked on a Tuesday and a Thursday.

Most forestry management work took place during the winter months. It focused on scrub clearance and clearing invasive plants such as rhododendron. During the summer, the probationers were split into smaller groups, with some working individually or in pairs, due to the changing nature of the work required. The scheme was flexible, allowing work to be completed in blocks of five days to reduce their community service time more quickly, but it also meant that tasks were seen through to their completion.

The teams used their own tools. The role of Forestry Commission staff was to identify the work, demonstrate new tasks and explain health and safety issues. All work on the placement was risk assessed by the Forestry Commission and the probation service. The O&N scheme kept track of all the work carried out. It recorded any problems and issues, so that they could be addressed and resolved.

This O&N scheme had several skilled joiners or builders among its number so they were able to get involved in construction tasks and decorating the visitor centre and teaching rooms.

Service provider

The Forestry Commission is the government department responsible for protecting, expanding and promoting the sustainable management of woodland and increasing their value to society and the environment.

Origins of the programme

The Forestry Commission has been running unpaid work schemes since the 1990s although many more schemes have been running since 2004. The impetus came from two sources: arson incidents in forests by local young people and approaches from the prison and probation services to find work for their clients.

Funding

The Forestry Commission is the major funder with additional funding from NOMS (see glossary). Most schemes have secured funding for the next two or three years.

Costs of the schemes vary, however it is estimated that it costs £17,500 per offender per annum. This cost includes the purchase of protective clothing, tools and equipment; transport; training; supervision and mentoring; project management and planning; and health and safety auditing.

Target group

The projects work with young people and adults on community sentences requiring a community payback (see glossary) element. Typically clients are between 16 and 50 years of age, however some participants have been as young as 12 years. The ratio of male:female is 4:1.

Referrals can be made from a wide geographical area, but the link to the local environment is encouraged. People are encouraged to connect and appreciate their local surroundings and also this helps build bridges between clients and 'mainstream' society.

Clients can be serving a community sentence or a prison sentence. Those entering O&N schemes during their community sentence are often working for one or two days per week on the scheme, whereas those serving a custodial sentence tend to participate full-time in the last six to nine months of their prison sentence. Prisoners participating in O&N projects are risk assessed to ensure that they can be released on temporary licence.

What does the programme do?

O&N initiatives involve partnerships between an offender-management organisation and a natural-environment organisation. O&N projects offer placements in line with the aims of the Home Office's 'Reducing Re-Offending Alliances' and the 'Community Payback' drive. The Forestry Commission's remit includes managing forests in a way that enables the public to experience, enjoy and benefit from wooded landscapes.

O&N schemes involve clients working as volunteers on nature conservation and woodland sites, carrying out tasks such as creating and maintaining footpaths, opening up dense vegetation to create more diverse habitats, establishing ponds and building boardwalks. They help address several key issues that can significantly affect reoffending: poor education; lack of employment; poor mental and physical health; problematic attitudes, thinking and behaviour; and lack of life skills.

Clients on community sentences usually work with O&N one or two days a week. The work has a reparative element, while it also provides experience of teamwork and life skills training aimed at boosting their confidence and self-esteem. The schemes offer physically demanding work in green space – numeracy, literacy and other academic skills are less relevant to the work than commitment, enthusiasm and diligence in following instructions by staff. Service users learn some basic conservation and forest management skills; get to know different tree, plant and animal species. Work often requires stamina and perseverance. Some supervisors observe a 'calming' and 'focusing' effect in volunteers. Days spent outside working in all weathers also improve physical fitness and a general feeling of wellbeing.

The scheme aims to:

- provide offenders with the opportunity to participate in outdoor, hands-on work placements that have multiple benefits;
- undertake enhancement work within the forest which would otherwise use scarce resources (cash/labour) or not get done due to resource constraints;
- give offenders the opportunity to learn basic conservation and forestry management skills;
- provide offenders with the opportunity to carry out work that is beneficial to society (community payback);
- provide a healthy environment for offenders to undertake their commitments;
- provide the interface between the public and offenders;
- introduce the forest environment to a wider audience;
- provide opportunities to disadvantaged groups; and
- reduce the incidence of inappropriate/anti-social behaviour in woodlands.

The work carried out is not just one project but many schemes, and while they share the aims and a basic set-up, each scheme also adapts and evolves from the specific local context and needs. Schemes for those on community sentences have a supervisor and transport provided by the probation service, so only limited training and supervisory input is needed from the Forestry Commission.

Some clients have realised that this type of work would suit them in the longer run and have applied for college courses, apprenticeships, or jobs in the same field. Some O&N schemes have offered short-term job opportunities to clients.

Client numbers

Since 2002, over 1,000 people participated across England in O&N schemes.

Staffing

The local or regional Forestry Commission offices will manage local O&N schemes. Strategies support and research is provided by a steering group which includes representatives from NOMS, the Home Office, Forestry Commission and Natural England.

Most schemes have a supervisor working with the clients on forest management tasks with support and input from a Forestry Commission manager and the regional manager. Overall each scheme has two or three people directly involved in the setting up, supporting and running of an O&N scheme.

Evaluation and effectiveness

Dartmoor Rehabilitation Project illustrates the success of this type of scheme. Since 2004, it has worked with 17 people on community orders. Nine have gone on to secure full-time employment, and four of those are employed in the tree and forestry sector. Others have secured outdoor careers in the building, fishing and water industries.

An internal appraisal of O&N projects suggests that they can have many profound and subtle impacts that benefit the offenders, the host organisation, the offender management institution and local communities.

Comments from foresters and conservationists working with young offenders illustrate this:

The description of the person when we took them and what they were like with us did not match. They worked well and were reliable.

You could tell a difference in them from when they started and when they finished working with us.

Graduates of the scheme have brought back relatives to show their work. One thanked staff on his O&N scheme:

Thank you for the opportunity it has given me in life that I may not have had. My time with the Forestry Commission has changed my outlook to life and work. I really believe for the first time I have a future.

Benefits of the scheme

Impacts and benefits of Offenders and Nature scheme

Beneficiary	Impacts and benefits
Nature provider' organisations	Ability to carry out work that is desirable but not done due to lack of resources (eg staff time unavailable or contractor costs high)
	Work completed to a high standard (due to enthusiasm and hands-on approach; more finished and refined look by using hand tools)
	Eco-systems improved through targeted management of habitats to favour diversity
	'Investing in People': providing an opportunity for disadvantaged people to gain work experience and training in the land based employment sector
	Nurturing a potential future workforce and volunteer base
	Increasing public awareness of investment in social forestry, nature conservation and public access to green space
	Broadening type and number of people using woodland and conservation sites

Beneficiary	Impacts and benefits
Prison and offender management	The prison delivering effective rehabilitation and reintegration opportunities to prisoners
	Large step forward for prisoners nearing end of their sentences, being granted release on licence to work outside prison
	Offenders carry out reparative work – repaying debt they owe to society
	Offenders have the opportunity to gain experience in a commercial but supportive environment, improving their employability after release
	Enabling offenders to develop personal skills (communication, team-working, endurance/stamina, decision-making)
	Duty of care to prisoners in terms of providing a healthy environment and staying in good health
	Building trust between prisoners and prison staff (offenders being reliable and willing to work and thereby gain respect)
	Positive thinking and experiences of prisoners; can affect other inmates and send a message of hope and opportunity
	Likelihood of re-offending lowered; hence successful rehabilitation and cost savings
	Multi-agency/partnership working with governmental and voluntary bodies to improve learning and skills of prisoners (in line with government green paper 2005 *Reducing re-offending through skills and employment*)

Beneficiary	Impacts and benefits
Offenders/ volunteers	Opportunity to test structured approach to working
	Opportunity to improve well-being and self-esteem through regular physical outdoor activity; also affects emotional stability and ability to adjust to life's demands
	Chance to experience restorative effects of woodlands and green spaces
	Opportunity to improve physical fitness and experience; other benefits of outdoor work (fresh air, pleasant surroundings)
	Chance to develop personal and interpersonal skills, awareness of health and safety issues, and safe approach to working in potentially hazardous environments
	Opportunity to develop decision-making skills while also having to receive and follow through instructions from others
	Learning new (transferable, technical) skills possibly gaining certificate/qualification through training
	Offenders being introduced to a range of potential jobs and further training opportunities
	Feeling physically tired after a hard day's work

Beneficiary	Impacts and benefits
Community	Areas are made lighter ad brighter (improved feeling of 'security')
	Improved 'aesthetics' of woodland and nature conservation areas (area 'looking tidier' is appreciated by most, though not all)
	Improved accessibility, better maintained paths
	Increased sightings of birds, butterflies and other attractive fauna and flora due to active conservation management practices
	Experiencing positive outcomes of 'punishment' system; for reparation and reconciliation
	Experiencing offenders as 'working people' and 'fellow human beings' (part of restorative process)
	Seeing people care for their local habitats and areas of recreation and amenity
	Movement towards more environmentally, socially and economically sustainable outcomes

Beneficiary	Impacts and benefits
Environment	More diverse woodlands and habitats
	Increased populations of common and rare fauna and flora due to active conservation management practices
	Restoration of neglected habitats

Source: Carter, C. (2007)

Contact details:

Claudia Carter
Social and Economic Research Group
Environmental and Human Sciences Division
Forest Research
Alice Holt Lodge
Farnham
Surrey
GU10 4LH

Tel: 01420 526191

E-mail: claudia.carter@forestry.gsi.gov.uk

The Community Service Unit Team (CSU), Dorset Probation Area

Scheme of special merit award 2007

A client's experience

'Mick' had been unemployed for 14 years. He was 44 years old and married. He was sentenced to a 120-hour community punishment order for assault and criminal damage.

During his induction process it was established that he needed to brush up on his literacy and numeracy skills, cognitive thinking skills and vocational skills learning. The Tank Museum at Bovington Camp was identified as an ideal placement. He was trained in engineering in the morning and basic skills in the afternoon.

Through the course he achieved Level 2 in both literacy and numeracy (the equivalent to GCSE grade 3) and an engineering certificate from Weymouth College. He worked extremely well during his order and had no unacceptable absences. He has been in work ever since.

Service provider

The CSU Team is made up of the Tank Museum at Bovington Camp; Weymouth College; the education, training and employment department (ETE) (see glossary) at Dorset probation service; and the community service unit at Wareham.

Origins of the programme and funding

The CSU has been involved with the Tank Museum since 2003. The Tank Museum needed help to clean and maintain its exhibits but had no funds to employ people, so the two teamed up.

Funding has been secured through the Learning and Skills Council.

Target group

The project targets people sentenced to community punishment orders with a UWO element. They are mainly aged 16 to 24 years. Many had been excluded from school before sitting their GCSEs. There is a minimum requirement of 100 hours UWO as the engineering module takes 13 weeks to complete. Also clients must not hold GCSE grade 3 in Maths and English.

What does the programme do?

The aim of the programme is to increase the employability and reduce reoffending by helping clients to attain Level 2 awards in literacy and numeracy and an engineering qualification. This project uses different partners to provide each component of the scheme. The Tank Museum offers engineering facilities and training to help offenders improve their life chances and employment opportunities. Weymouth College focuses on numeracy and literacy tuition. Two basic skills and one engineering tutor teach at the Tank Museum.

An initial on-screen assessment is undertaken by Weymouth College on those identified for the scheme. This assesses their current level of attainment and potential to progress. Selection for the scheme depends on this, an interview with their probation officer and a desire to obtain an engineering qualification.

Clients take part on the programme for seven hours per day, one day per week, in a group of no more than eight people. Every Wednesday clients attend the Tank Museum under the supervision of a probation supervisor, a workshop manager and two tutors from Weymouth College. The working environment aims to convey a good work ethic coupled with the knowledge and understanding of an orderly and safe workplace.

The group carries out engineering activities on some of the museum's exhibits through refurbishment of tanks, armoured cars and other vehicles. It involves a mixture of hands-on vocational learning in engineering, working in the workshop in the mornings on two-hour sessions, and classroom tuition on basic skills in the afternoons, in the Tank Museum library.

A report is written by the probation supervisor after each session, highlighting what clients have achieved during the session. These reports are sent back to the CSU. Clients' progress is ultimately measured by examinations entered and results gained at the end of the UWOs.

Client numbers

The CSU supervises approximately 350 offenders per week who are carrying out UWOs of between 40 and 300 hours. Over the last year, CSU has supervised over 80,000 unpaid work hours, which have benefited communities across Dorset.

Staffing

The team which oversees the project includes:

- CS unit manager;
- CS deputy manager;
- CS supervisor;
- Curator – the Tank Museum;
- Workshop manager – the Tank Museum;
- Weymouth College learning manager;
- ETE manager; and
- ETE deputy manager.

Evaluation and effectiveness

The CSU measures the success of the scheme through service users' attainment of qualifications. Since 2003, clients have gained 15 engineering qualifications and 137 literacy and numeracy qualifications, of which 50 were at Level 2. Only one person out of the 137 has been reconvicted of another offence. Several clients have gained employment as a result of their experience at the Tank Museum.

Benefits of the scheme

Mike Mathews, deputy unit manager at Dorset Probation Area told the Howard League for Penal Reform:

The Tank Museum, Weymouth College and the Dorset Probation Service have given offenders the opportunity to achieve commercially recognised awards in engineering, English and maths. The partnership has been of great benefit to the museum in securing them 1,800 hours of free labour. Offenders have been benefiting from these experiences and tuition from Weymouth College, which is allowing some to gain employment for the first time in years. In return, the museum has assistance in keeping the vehicles and exhibits clean, and others can be renovated for use in live demonstrations.

This scheme builds service users' self-esteem by helping them to achieve something which many of them have never had before – a qualification. Some of them had been told they were 'thick' at school and not to bother turning up to sit the exams. This was the case for one service user who cried when he was presented with his Level 2 numeracy certificate. It was the first certificate he had ever had in his life. He had achieved something he was told he would never ever get.

Contact details:

Mike Matthews
Deputy Manager
The Community Service Unit
19 Sandford Lane
Wareham
BH20 4JH

Tel: 01929 556513

Email: Mike.Matthews@dorset.probation.gsi.gov.uk

CHAPTER 8

High-Risk Offenders

The term 'high-risk offenders' refers to those people who have been convicted of a sexual and/or violent offence and present a degree of potential harm to the public. Public protection is a primary consideration when working with high-risk offenders, but this does not preclude community programmes being provided and effectively delivered. The greater level of monitoring that is developed when working with this group in many ways can be regarded as enhancing public protection.

Appropriate accommodation alongside good communication and information sharing between key agencies are essential if this group is going to be managed effectively. Both these facets are reflected in the work of Staffordshire Intensive Floating Support Scheme.

The voluntary sector is often at the forefront of innovation. This is particularly true with the work to support high-risk offenders using Circles of Support and Accountability. In this scheme, support is offered in addition to, and not instead of, statutory controls on the offender to protect the public. This project is based on a Canadian initiative designed to support the safe integration of sex offenders into the community. The scheme trains carefully selected volunteers to support and hold offenders to account. The whole emphasis of Circles of Support and Accountability is on including, rather than excluding: thereby providing a real and meaningful community for a group of people who tended to be stigmatised and marginalised.

Intensive Floating Support Scheme for High-Risk Offenders (IFSS), Staffordshire Probation Area and Heantun Housing Association (HHA)

Scheme of special merit award 2005

A client's experience

'Adam' was in his early 20s. Approximately one year ago he was charged with possession of indecent images and given a community order. His probation conditions included attending both the community sex offender group and the alcohol addiction support group (Aquarius).

Adam's probation officer made a referral to our service with the aim of trying to improve his economic wellbeing, social activities and networks, employment and/or training opportunities and seeking independent living.

At the time of being referred to our service Adam was nervous but enthusiastic about getting involved with the public protection liaison officer (PPLO) service. He informed us that his hope was to move out of his parent's house, get a full-time job and thus manage his finances better, and try to control the amount of alcohol he consumed.

Adam was living with his parents, and had no other social contacts as many of his friends had ended their friendship after finding out about his conviction. His social isolation was having a great impact on his emotional wellbeing and led to a lack of self-worth and confidence and often led to him feeling depressed. As a means of coping he would frequent pubs in the hope of making new friends and 'drown his sorrows'. All these factors would impact on his motivation to seek his goals. Adam spent the majority of his days sleeping and listening to music, and drinking in the local pubs.

In the early visits we discussed his lack of motivation and we started to set small goals which were perfectly achievable, such as looking through the employment section of local newspapers and enquiring whether he was eligible for jobs he was interested in, completing a CV and budgeting his finances. When it became apparent to Adam that he could achieve his goals when he put his mind to it, it encouraged him to act more independently and set larger goals.

After approximately four months of working towards seeking independent living by completing various housing applications and getting Adam to budget his finances, he was offered his own property. His pleasure at this move forward in his life seemed at first to elicit a more open response to my discussions about his increasing alcohol consumption and Adam become more determined to reduce his consumption. This was an extremely positive move forward as the hardest part in many ways had been convincing Adam that he didn't need to rely on alcohol when life became difficult.

Adam had never lived independently and thus he lacked some of the skills to do so. The frequency of visits were increased as he needed support and guidance to help develop these life and social skills and needed encouragement to do things independently, such as contacting the housing authority to make repairs to the property and setting up payment plans for his household bills.

Soon after moving into his own accommodation Adam was also offered employment, which he readily accepted. Through working full-time his self-esteem has grown considerably and he has started to develop healthy adult relationships, which don't revolve around alcohol.

When Adam was eventually made redundant, however, he showed a more mature, confident and independent attitude. He immediately contacted the relevant bodies to secure continual financial help so that his tenancy wouldn't be affected and registered with various employment agencies. He was able to regain employment and has developed a strong work ethic. His sense of self-worth has increased dramatically over the past nine months.

Adam continues his work with the Aquarius probation officer and has made good progress. He stated that he drunk a lot less due to the consequences it may have on his freedom and health, and due to the implications it may have for his tenancy. Adam also managed his finances better and has saved a reasonable amount in case he ever became unemployed again. Adam was extremely motivated and enthusiastic towards the future and talked about similar goals each time I saw him.

Service provider

Staffordshire Probation Area and Heantun Housing Association jointly deliver IFFS.

Origins of the programme

Staffordshire Probation Area established IFSS in 2002. It was designed to meet new statutory responsibilities for the monitoring and management of dangerous offenders in the community following the introduction of the Criminal Justice and Court Services Act 2000.

Traditionally, local authorities and housing providers have been reluctant to provide accommodation to this client group. This meant approved premises (see glossary) were often filled with a static high-risk population. This scheme has helped secure and maintain stable accommodation in the community for high-risk offenders, while still providing an increased level of support and surveillance.

Funding

Staffordshire and Stoke on Trent Supporting People Grant (see glossary) funded the scheme. Heantun Housing Association (HHA) has successfully tendered to deliver the service until March 2009.

The scheme costs around £70,000 per year, plus around £2,000 associated costs for the probation service.

Target group

The scheme is for clients under current probation supervision who are under Staffordshire MAPPA (see glossary). The following criteria apply:

- referrals must come from probation officers;
- clients must be from Staffordshire;
- clients must be currently or in the process of being registered with MAPPA;
- all potential clients must be subject to a community rehabilitation order (see glossary), community punishment and rehabilitation order, or be on post-release licence supervision (see glossary) (non-statutory cases can, however, be considered if there are strong reasons for a PPLO's (see glossary) involvement);
- clients must have been assessed by Staffordshire probation as being motivated and willing to comply with PPLO involvement; and
- clients must have been assessed as being able to benefit from PPLO involvement.

What does the programme do?

This programme supports Staffordshire multi-agency public protection panels (MAPPPs) by delivering an enhanced level of support and surveillance to high-risk offenders who have been assessed as requiring additional support with resettlement and housing in the community. The aim is to help clients to maintain appropriate accommodation in the community; to ensure that the conditions and requirements of supervision plans/licences are adhered to; and to reduce the risk of offending.

HHA employs PPLOs to support and monitor clients in the community, providing them with housing advice;

intensive housing management support; assistance and support with life and social skills development; and assistance and support with employment and/or training.

PPLOs make regular visits to the client in their accommodation. The frequency of these visits is determined by a support plan. The PPLO develops this plan in consultation with the client's case manager and the client. It is based on the identified needs and risks. Visits are normally once per week, once per fortnight or once per month. The visits are normally pre-arranged, however, unannounced visits will be made, especially if there are concerns about the client's behaviour, for example developing inappropriate new friendships. If necessary, work will be undertaken well above the agreed involvement and in exceptional cases, contact has been made on a daily basis. PPLOs' visits are usually made in office hours. Exceptions will be made, for example, when clients are in employment or undergoing training. Visits last between one and two hours.

Client visit protocol

The PPLO referral form indicates whether client visits require two people to attend due to perceived risk factors. Regardless of the risk, the first visit with the client is always undertaken in conjunction with the supervising probation officer.

The PPLO line manager is kept informed of all planned visits and given full details of the visit. It is essential that PPLOs inform a specified designated person, shortly before going on a visit. This designated person will have all the details of who they are visiting, at what address, a clear time for when the visit should have ended and a mobile contact number.

Once the visit finishes, the PPLO contacts the specified person to advise them that they are safe. Should no contact be made after five minutes of the scheduled end of the visit, the designated person will contact the PPLO. If there is no response then the specified person would contact the police and ask for support.

Client numbers

Each PPLO supports up to 15 clients. The service has a maximum capacity of 30 clients. The project has worked with 50 service users during the period from January to December 2007. The average length of involvement per case is 259 days, yet it has ranged from 42 to 490 days.

Monitoring

PPLOs write a report, using a standard format, after each visit. It is submitted to their line manager, the client's case manager, and others as specified by MAPPA. Any immediate concerns are passed on to the case manager and other relevant agencies by telephone. Close liaison is maintained with the client's case manager, particularly if the client fails to make an appointment.

Staffing

The project is overseen and monitored through the Staffordshire IFSS Management Group, with representatives from the probation service, the police, accommodation officers, bail hostels and HHA. Day-to-day management and supervision of the scheme is provided by three full-time PPLOs and a manager employed under service level agreement with HHA.

Benefits of the scheme

IFSS has identified numerous benefits of the scheme to clients, the public, and in enhancing the work undertaken by local agencies.

Benefits to clients:

- practical support with the aim of preventing offending;
- reduces isolation and increases support; and
- provides stable accommodation which would otherwise be difficult to access and retain.

Benefits to the public:

- increased surveillance; and
- agencies can provide greater protection through a better understanding of risks posed by the client group.

Benefits to local agencies:

- an increased level of support from PPLOs enabling them to provide more support in their specialist area;
- frees up space in approved premises;
- increases surveillance of high-risk offenders and the possibility of early warning potential of reoffending; and
- provides additional monitoring which cements multi-agency working to enhance the risk-management system

Volunteers

The scheme does not currently use volunteers, although the model employed by Circles of Support and Accountability (see below) is being considered. This innovation would enable IFSS to provide extra support and monitoring outside traditional office hours.

Evaluation and effectiveness

Staff and clients complete internal evaluation forms about the service provided and its impact.

C.A. Reed Management and Consultancy, an independent management and consultancy group, evaluated the scheme in 2004. It concluded that the scheme runs and works effectively (Reed 2004). Of the 41 cases assessed by the evaluation only one client has reoffended after moving to a new area, outside Staffordshire.

Contact details:

Joy Wright
Area Manager
Heantun Housing Association
Wellington House
3 Wellington Road
Bilston
Wolverhampton
WV14 6AA

Tel: 01902 571 100

Email: Joy.Wright@heantun.co.uk

Circles of Support and Accountability (Circles), Hampshire and Thames Valley, Oxfordshire

Scheme of special merit award 2006

A client's experience

'Peter' was 61 years old and single. In November 2002 he was sentenced to a sex offender order. His offences related to child pornography. He had befriended children. He has also been seen outside a school watching children and had children's paraphernalia (toys/underpants) in his car. Peter had previous convictions for unlawful sexual intercourse, abduction and indecent assault of a child, and four cases of indecent assault.

As Peter had a low IQ he had never undertaken any formal sex offender treatment programme (SOTP).

A number of factors meant that Peter was an ideal candidate to be a core circle member. He was a predatory offender with clear paedophilic tendencies. Peter quickly sexualised situations involving young children. He had a number of previous convictions and a high-risk status. He had an unstable lifestyle compounded by his homelessness. In addition to placing Peter at the centre of a circle, the probation service authorised a place in an approved premises, despite no order to facilitate this being in place, and Peter was tagged.

When Peter's circle formed, circle volunteers immediately became aware that Peter needed a lot of practical support. For instance, Peter's order stipulated he was not to go within 40 yards of a playground. Peter had absolutely no idea how far this was and so was in danger of breaching his order. In order for Peter to move on from the hostel, the circle tried to find sheltered housing for him, as he clearly did not have the resources to look after himself at this time. When accommodation was found, the warden was trained by Circles' staff, as an added precaution so that he was risk-aware.

Three months into Peter's tenancy the warden found him with three girls in his flat. They were aged between 6 and 24 years. This was regarded as highly risky behaviour, particularly in view of the age and vulnerability of the youngest girl. It was also clear that they were regular visitors who were given cigarettes as gifts. Peter was found to be in breach of his order. In 2005, he was sentenced to a probation order for three years and returned to the hostel.

In 2006, a new circle was formed for Peter with a new set of volunteers. This circle used some methods outlined in the Adapted SOTP which is specifically designed for people with learning difficulties. An aim was to enhance Peter's victim empathy and to help him design a workable relapse prevention strategy.

The circle formally closed in May 2007. Peter had independent accommodation; he was in suitable employment and he had been helped to manage his finances. Two circle members continued with fortnightly contact to monitor his mood and specifically a relationship that he was developing with a woman on the Internet.

This case offers a good example of the management of a high-risk and high-need sexual offender in the community through inter-agency work. Although Circles cannot be sure that he has not reoffended, he has not been reconvicted.

Service provider

Hampshire and Thames Valley Circles of Support & Accountability began in 2002 as a government pilot project managed by the Religious Society of Friends (Quakers). It is community initiative working in partnership with the police, probation and prison services and is funded by the Ministry of Justice. On the 1st April 2008 the project was launched as an independent charitable company with the Quakers handing over full responsibility to the Board of Trustees.

Origins of the programme

Circles of Support and Accountability have existed in Canada for ten years. They were designed to support and reintegrate sex offenders who were released from prison back into the community. Quakers brought the idea to England. Quakers have been developing and promoting Circles and a pilot project has been running in the Thames Valley area since 2002 and in Hampshire since 2005.

Circles is currently encouraging and supporting the development of projects around the country, in particular Somerset, Yorkshire, Norfolk, Manchester, Bedfordshire and Scotland. Other organisations, including the Lucy Faithful Foundation, are also running similar projects. On the 1st April 2008 Circles UK, the new national umbrella organisation launched as an independent charitable company. It will provide all projects with support and training to ensure the quality and consistency of the work.

Funding

Funding initially came from the NPS and then from NOMS (see glossary). Circles is working towards obtaining a charitable status in 2008.

Funding is currently £320,000 per year.

Target group

Men and women who have been convicted of any sexual offence who are due to be released from prison are eligible.

Additional criteria for a core member to join a circle:

- high-risk/need which is assessed on a case-by-case basis;
- voluntary agreement to join a circle;
- due to start or complete accredited SOTP (see glossary) group work in the community;

- indication of accepting of responsibility for actions and is motivated to stop offending;
- socially isolated; and
- living in the local area.

Referrals

Once a potential core member has been identified the Circles co-ordinator assesses their suitability. The assessment is aided by the results of a psychometric test and information from the police and probation services.

What does the programme do?

Circles supports the re-integration of sex offenders released from prison back into the community, while at the same time holding them accountable for their actions. It provides a structured restorative approach for working with high-risk and high need offenders.

A circle is formed with the released prisoner at its centre (core member). Volunteers who represent the local community and professionals, who will only attend when necessary, form the circle of support and accountability.

A circle:

- is a group of trained volunteers (usually four for each circle) recruited from the community;
- is set up at the request of the sex offender who wants to stop offending;
- works alongside others, such as a family member, police and probation services; and
- is made up of volunteers supported and supervised by appropriate professionals throughout the period of contact with the core member.

Circles are vehicles to address the issues regarding victims, offenders and community need. This can only be achieved if the core member is committed to accepting the circle's assistance and guidance, and promises that 'there will be no more victims at my hand'.

A circle is about:

- helping a core member to reintegrate responsibly into the community;
- enhancing public safety when there is a perceived element of risk; and
- acting as a support and safety mechanism for both the core member and the community.

A circle will meet regularly, initially weekly, for a formal circle meeting. These meetings will, over time, become less frequent, moving to fortnightly and then monthly. It is often when the circle moves to fortnightly meetings that individual contact rather than just group contact by volunteers begins with the core member. The work of the circle is monitored by a Circles co-ordinator.

Formal meetings will take place in an appropriate public environment like a café or restaurant. This needs to be a safe environment that will allow the core member to discuss problematic and sensitive issues confidentially.

The circle becomes 'informal' when the circle co-ordinator (a staff member) and all members of the circle recognise and agree the time is right. This usually happens between 12 and 18 months after the circle started. The frequency of meetings is then reduced. An informal circle will focus on social activities and individual progress rather than on specific work linked to the core member's offending behaviour. This is to facilitate independence. It also reduces the core member's dependency on the circle.

Very few circles are completely discontinued, as the core members tend to continue contact with volunteers.

Closures, when they do occur, tend to be when a core member:

- moves to a new area;
- successfully achieves all that they can and can stand independently in the community;
- requests an end of a circle;
- is recalled to prison;
- stops attending circle meetings and engaging with volunteers; or
- commits a new sexual offence and receives a custodial sentence.

A circle can be re-formed if a core member experiences problematic situations and requires the support of the circle on a regular basis for period of time. Circles are also restructured, if, for example, a volunteer wants to stop volunteering but the circle still needs to continue. The circle will then be restructured to provide the continued support. New volunteers can be introduced to the circle.

Client numbers

There have been 40 circles in the past five years. At the moment there are 21 active circles.

Staffing

The Circles project manager became the new charity's Chief Executive on the 1st April. There are also three full-time circles co-ordinators, an office manager and a sessional assistant psychologist. Circles also has the use of the Thames Valley Police forensic psychologist.

Circles employs professional trainers for the annual volunteer training programme.

Circles reports to a steering group consisting of key partner agencies including the probation and police services and the Thames Valley Partnership.

Circles also has a volunteer action group to advise the project manager.

Volunteers

Circle volunteers are recruited, screened and trained to support and hold accountable, core circle members. Volunteers work individually and as a team.

Circle volunteers are not intended to replace or undermine the role of professionals working with offenders. Instead Circles complement and support the work of statutory partners. People commit to being a volunteer for at least a year. However, Circles' experience shows that original volunteers who start with a core member stay with the circle. Some circles have been running for five years. There have been over 100 volunteers with Circles.

Potential volunteers will attend an initial two-day training event which looks at the role of Circles. It is designed to help volunteers decide whether Circles is right for them. A Circles co-ordinator will also assess an individual's suitability to be a volunteer. If selected, references are taken up and a CRB (see glossary) check undertaken. Sexual abuse survivors have been selected as volunteers.

Following selection, volunteers receive extensive training. The following sessions are completed:

- professional workshop – looking at the role and relationship between Circles and police, probation, MAPPA (see glossary);
- media training – equip volunteers with knowledge they required to handle difficult encounters with the press;
- booster days – mandatory training designed for volunteers who have worked in a circle for more than a year;

- housing training – looking at legal issues, grants and deposits, housing providers, benefits and keeping tenancy;
- substance misuse training;
- working with female sex offenders; and
- questioning styles and techniques – enables volunteers to develop helping skills and to understand the importance of listening, guidance and instruction.

In order to support volunteers, personal reviews are undertaken every three months once they are placed in a circle. In addition, a review may take place at any time at the request of either the volunteer or the co-ordinator. Volunteers are encouraged to telephone staff for advice or support as it is needed.

Evaluation and effectiveness

Information from Circles shows that:

- no core member has been convicted of a new sexual offence in the past five years;
- only one core member has been convicted of a new offence: attempted burglary;
- one core member has been convicted for breach of a sex offence prevention order;
- three core members have been recalled to prison following breach of their parole licence; and
- in four cases, recidivist behaviour by a core member has been identified by their circle. This information was passed to the local multi-agency risk manager. The core member was also held to account within the circle.

Quaker Peace and Social Witness (QPSW) undertook an evaluation of Circles' first three years (Quaker Peace and Social Witness 2005). The evaluation reflects the vast amount of 'soft data' that Circles has provided about recidivist behaviours in sex offenders and their experiences and challenges when living in the community, crime free, with the support of a circle, among other things. The evaluation also highlights that Circles is as much about accountability as it is about supporting core members. The evaluation found that long entrenched behaviours often lead to a resurgence of illegal behaviour (for example, recidivism). In these situations, the input provided by Circles often led to vital information which either triggered recall or other offence-limiting strategies that, in turn, enhanced public protection. The Circles process provided unique insights into core members' behaviours and lifestyles, well beyond that garnered through statutory supervision.

The evaluation highlighted how Circles enhanced public protection by identifying behaviour that might have previously gone unchecked. In one case, a circle found its core member was grooming girls aged under 16 years in Internet chat rooms, which resulted in the core member's recall to prison. This suggests that circles facilitate early intervention and the vital role that Circles can have in managing the risk posed by dangerous sex offenders in the community.

Contact details:

Rebeckah Saunders
Director
Circles of Support and Accountability
Hampshire and Thames Valley
140a Broadway
Didcot
Oxfordshire
OX11 8RJ

Tel: 01235 816050

Email: becky.circles@btconnect.com

CHAPTER 9

Resettlement

Community programmes that support prisoners on release from prison have also been recognised by the Howard League for Penal Reform's Community Programmes Award. The inclusion of these programmes highlights the importance that should be placed on ensuring that resettlement arrangements are put in place before the end of a sentence and the need for continuity of support into the community. Unfortunately research has shown that all too often this resettlement work is at best piecemeal and inadequately co-ordinated (Nacro 2005; The Howard League for Penal Reform 2006).

All prisoners should have an individual resettlement strategy that addresses issues to help them lead a crime-free life, including housing, education, employment and welfare support. Ideally this should be a well-organised seamless service that starts at the prison gate and continues post-release into the community.

The Transitional Support Scheme (TSS) is an example of a project working closely with short-term prisoners (serving less than 12 months) before and after they are released into the community, helping with their resettlement plans and needs. The Howard League for Penal Reform's (2007) research showed that short custodial sentences result in a reconviction rate of 73% within two years of release from prison. We believe that services targeted to meet the needs of this client group are crucial in addressing and reducing reoffending behaviour, and ultimately protecting the public from more crime.

TSS provides 'through the gate' mentoring support for prisoners on release. The mentors help clients to define personal goals, set realistic targets and establish what professional assistance they require to support their rehabilitation. The individual support of specialist and committed mentors helps to ensure that prisoners can succeed on release from prison.

Transitional Support Scheme (TSS), Group 4 Justice Services (G4S), South Wales and Gwent Areas

Outstanding scheme award 2006

A client's experience

'Kerry' was in and out of prison since he committed his first offence at the age of 19 years. He was serving a seven-month prison sentence for deception when he came into contact with TSS. He had obtained credit cards because he needed the money. He was homeless prior to the offence. Kerry said that prior to the offence, he did not have much contact with his family and had only been getting on with his father over the past five years.

Kerry told us: 'I first heard about TSS at a resettlement fair at Parc prison. My mentor explained the scheme to me and I thought that this was a good way to help me'. Initially, Kerry thought that the scheme would be similar to the supervision from a probation officer when released on licence and he also said that he was not looking forward to it. But, after a few meetings with his mentor, he realised that the purpose of the scheme was to offer him support during a time of change. Kerry said: 'I looked forward to my appointments with my mentor as I felt that she was also someone I could talk to. She helped me with my housing situation and I am now living in a bed and breakfast. She also told me about where I could go to receive financial support'.

Kerry said that the TSS experience was beneficial to him and he would definitely recommend the scheme to friends. He said that the best part of the scheme was the motivational support that he received from his mentor.

Service provider

G4S is one of the first private sector providers of such a scheme. It delivers the service in partnership with the Welsh Assembly Government and the prison and probation services.

Origins of the programme and funding

The Welsh Assembly Government funded TSS following recognition that there was little or no resettlement support for prisoners released from a short prison sentence. Short sentenced prisoners receive no statutory supervision on release. It was launched in January 2004. There are two TSS projects in Wales. In North Wales it is delivered by the DAWN project which is a partnership initiative led by CAIS (a drug and alcohol agency based in Llandudno). G4S provides the service in South Wales and Gwent, and is based outside Parc Prison in Bridgend

TSS has secured funding until December 2010.

Target group

Service users are introduced to the scheme through a wide range of channels, although generally through the counselling, assessment, referral, advice and throughcare (CARAT) team (see glossary), a programme tutor or the prisoner resettlement teams, prison staff, the local DTTO (see glossary) office or self-referral.

The scheme is voluntary and in order to qualify for TSS support, prisoners must:

- be relocating to Wales;
- be serving a prison sentence of less than 12 months; and
- have a substance misuse/alcohol problem.

What does the programme do?

TSS aims to provide 'through the gate' mentoring support for prisoners serving less than 12 months who are returning to live in Wales.

At Parc Prison prisoners are invited to attend a resettlement fair one month before they are released. The fair is attended by external support agencies, housing agencies, and drug and alcohol agencies. Employers and recruitment agencies are present to offer advice and arrange appointments post-release. TSS is also at these fairs to attract referrals onto their scheme.

Generally referrals are made to TSS several weeks prior to a prisoner's release date. Prison probation staff will risk assess them before they are accepted onto TSS. TSS staff have access to the offender assessment system (OASys) (see glossary) and can use it to obtain more information about clients before they take part on the project.

Following acceptance onto the scheme the TSS staff profiler will design a package for each client and assign a mentor. Clients and mentors are 'matched' in terms of interests, personality, gender and geography.

Mentors help clients to define personal goals, set realistic targets and establish what professional assistance they require to support their rehabilitation. TSS offers up to 12 weeks support following release from custody. It is voluntary and participants refer themselves.

TSS is designed to address the practical resettlement needs. The primary focus is on securing access to drug treatment and subsequently reduction and/or cessation of drug use. TSS also focuses on homelessness; relationship problems; finances; low educational attainment; and unemployment.

Mentors are used to enhance the motivation of service users to address their offending behaviour through the application of cognitive and motivational techniques. They will meet clients to provide reassurance and motivation to change. The scheme is about providing support and guidance rather than advice to its service users. Clients are linked up with professionals and agencies. The mentors support their clients in working with the agencies, to try and break down any barriers that may exist in accessing services and to negotiate the bureaucracies of the agencies.

Once in the community, the mentor will visit the client, explore and discuss what issues need to be addressed to support them in the community. A mentor could, for example, meet the client at their current address, then take them to visit the housing department to help out with securing housing, then to the benefits office, or look at referral on to drugs agencies.

The work of TSS has shown that many of the clients do not have money or transport. This often makes it difficult to access the help and support they need. For example, their temporary accommodation may be in a different town from their probation office, housing department or drugs service, so the mentor will help get them to their appointments and support them in maintaining contact.

Contact with clients usually comes to an end after 12 weeks. If clients are doing well and are working well with partner agencies it is possible to leave TSS before the end of 12 weeks.

There is an established exit strategy for mentors, which prepares clients for ending their contact with their mentor by reducing the frequency of visits and meetings. Both the mentor and client will agree on a date to end contact but the client will know that they can call the scheme and even come back to the scheme if they feel they require more support.

Client protocol

Initially the mentor will visit their client in prison where they will introduce themselves and also provide further information on TSS. Initial meetings in the prison are used to build a rapport in preparation for their work in the community. Mentors work on their own with clients unless the risk assessment is such that two mentors are allocated; however, this is unusual.

On the client's prison release date the mentor will meet them at the prison gate and take them to their secured accommodation and help them to settle in. Subsequent visits will take place either at the client's home or in public places.

After each visit to a client the mentor must check in with another member of staff using a buddy system. They have to make a telephone call to notify them of their safety. They can also call the TSS co-ordinator on an hourly basis if out on many visits. Each mentor calls the office at the end of the day for a check in. All mentors are supplied with TSS equipment to carry during community contacts, which includes a mobile phone, first aid kit and personal attack alarm.

A contact sheet is completed by the mentor after each visit or telephone conversation. This is used to monitor the level of contact, the amount of work carried out, the interventions suggested and the client's progress.

If a client misses an appointment a letter is sent reminding them that they missed an appointment and asking them to make contact to arrange another appointment. If the client does not contact TSS within the following seven days a second letter is sent. This process is followed once more. If there is still no contact from the client a third and final letter is sent to close the case unless the client makes contact again.

Client numbers in the last year

Since the project started in January 2004, TSS has worked with 883 men and 78 women. There are usually 90 cases open at any one time.

Staffing

TSS uses a mix of full-time staff and mentors, many of whom are drawn from the existing staff of Parc Prison. The scheme staff structure is:

- one manager;
- one supervisor;
- one profiler/administrator;
- eight TSS full-time paid mentors;
- one prison Connexions (see glossary) worker;
- a minimum of two university placement students (second year criminology/psychology); and
- volunteers (variable in numbers).

A project management board, made up of representatives from the Welsh Assembly Government, the prison and probation services, oversees TSS.

Mentor training and support

G4S has devised and delivered its own training package for TSS mentors. It has accreditation from the National Mentoring Network (see glossary). It is designed to be flexible and takes into account the differing abilities and experience of new staff. It focuses on equipping TSS mentors with sufficient knowledge and confidence to work effectively with clients. The training provides a theoretical background for motivational work with offenders; a record of G4S TSS mentor policy documents and field paperwork; a voluntary and statutory agency referral directory; plus an overview of the changing legislation and practice as it relates to the effectiveness and implementation of the scheme.

Newly recruited mentors with no previous experience of mentoring and who have never worked with offenders are required to complete the full training package.

Every three months, full-time mentors have a supervision session with the TSS manager and they also attend monthly mentor support groups with all staff members. These are held after the end of the working day to accommodate all those working at TSS. Team meetings are held every week for permanent TSS staff.

Volunteers

TSS is committed to user involvement in the delivery and monitoring of its service. It has established a peer advisory panel (PAP) made up of successful TSS service users who are volunteers. They provide valuable input, advice and guidance on the way the service is running. The PAP meets on a regular basis to discuss the TSS processes and provide a critical overview of the scheme. PAP members will also represent TSS and liaise with other agencies, including the police, support groups and prison CARAT teams. They visit participants to the scheme with mentors and also promote the scheme to ex-offenders to make referrals to TSS.

TSS also recruits university students to work as volunteers. They are usually second year criminology or psychology students on placements. They are provided with mentoring training. The students provide mentoring and administrative support, liaise with internal and external agencies, support groups, police services, and visit prisoners to discuss TSS issues.

Effectiveness and benefits of the scheme

The TSS approach to mentoring is unique. It is much more person focused. It is based on instilling motivation and self-esteem in the people the mentors are working with by building individual's confidence and beliefs in their own ability to achieve change. Clients are encouraged to take responsibility for their own actions rather than being led to change.

Staff are an important element to the effective operation of TSS. They form a professional team that is passionate about its work and delivering a mentoring programme it believes in. Some staff have also been through the same issues that TSS is helping to resolve for clients. G4S believes the mixture of leadership, staff experience, commitment and belief in the service users makes for an effective scheme.

Monitoring and evaluation

The Welsh Assembly Government commissioned a 12-month evaluation in May 2004 (Clancy et al. 2004). It found that G4S was the only provider which had achieved statistically significant results in changing the attitudes of participants. It suggested that: *'this may well be explained by the increased focus amongst G4S staff on the use of motivational enhancement techniques and the need to address offenders' motivation to change … the greater focus in the G4S training for TSS staff to concentrate on the clients' motivation, increased the post release contact rate'.*

The evaluation assessed prisoners' profiles, their attitudes to crime and the level of practical and emotional problems they faced. Each was given a score. Prisoners on the TSS scheme managed by G4S typically showed a high severity of life problems and with an equally above-average degree of pro-criminogenic attitudes. Many also had to arrange accommodation and employment after release and in some cases had to deal with the police about outstanding offences, which the evaluation stated could easily erode motivation for change. The introduction of a mentor provided a highly valued support.

The evaluation also highlighted:

- significant positive differences in attitude between pre- and post-mentoring;
- 67% service uptake; and
- 69% of participants reported that their mentor had had a positive effect upon their drug use post release.

G4S is also required to provide quantitative data to the project management board, and data up to 30 June 2006 showed:

- 474 referrals to the TSS since January 2004;
- an average of 432 mentor contact hours per quarter; and
- 624 contacts within the prison environment and 4,065 community-based contacts.

Contact details:

Sandy Phillips
TSS Manager South Wales & Gwent Area
Group 4 Securicor Justice Services
1 Parc Cottages
Heol Hopcyn John
Bridgend
Mid Glamorgan, South Wales
CF35 6AR

Tel: 01656 300278

E-Mail: sandy.phillips@uk.g4s.com

Glossary

Approved premises

Approved premises provide controlled accommodation for offenders under the supervision of the probation service.

Arrest referral service

The arrest referral service is an initiative whereby a dedicated drugs worker at the police station refers drug using arrestees to appropriate treatment. Involvement in the scheme is voluntary.

Asset

Asset is a structured assessment tool used by YOTs in England and Wales on all young people who have offended and come into contact with the criminal justice system. It collates information on factors that may contribute to offending behaviour like poor education or mental health problems. The information is used by courts to put together sentences and to help deliver the sentence effectively.

CARAT team (counselling, assessment, referral, advice and throughcare)

The CARAT service was established in 1999 as a universal drug treatment service in every prison establishment across England and Wales. Prisoners are assessed, advised and referred to appropriate drug services. CARAT workers may also offer counselling and group work to prisoners.

Child and adolescent mental health service (CAMHS)

CAMHS promotes the mental health and psychological wellbeing of its client group and provides high-quality, multi-disciplinary mental health services to ensure effective assessment, treatment and support, for the clients and their families.

The Children's Fund

The Children's Fund is a government initiative launched in November 2000 to tackle disadvantage among children and young people. It encouraged voluntary organisations, community and faith groups to work in partnership with local statutory agencies to deliver high-quality preventative services to meet the needs of communities.

Child protection register

Every local authority is required to maintain a register of children in its area who are thought to be at continuing risk of significant harm and therefore in need of protection by the authority. There are four categories: neglect; physical abuse; sexual abuse; and emotional abuse. Children are placed on the register following a child protection conference.

Community order

The community order was introduced in April 2005 under the Criminal Justice Act 1998. It replaced all existing community sentences for offences committed from April 2005. It enabled sentencers to tailor-make a community sentence to suit individual needs choosing from a range of 12 different requirements.

Community Payback

Provides the opportunity for local people to have their say on how men and women who have committed crimes should make amends for the harm they have caused.

Community rehabilitation order

A court order that required offenders to be supervised by the probation service. It may have conditions attached which require offenders to attend group work, reside at specific addresses, or participate in particular activities.

Community sports leaders award

An award designed for people aged over 16 years who wish to acquire confidence and ability in organising groups in games and physical recreation.

Connexions

The government's support service for all young people aged 13 to 19 years in England. It provides support for young people with learning difficulties or disabilities up to the age of 25 years. It uses a multi-agency approach to provide information, advice, and guidance and to facilitate access to personal development opportunities for young people.

Construction skills certification scheme

The construction industry's biggest scheme covering all trades, supervisors and managers. It registers everyone who is competent to work in construction. It is a requirement that most contractors and clients now demand.

Criminal Records Bureau (CRB)

An executive agency of the Home Office that provides a disclosure service for criminal records information. It may be accessed by the public, private and voluntary sectors through established mechanisms. CRB was established under Part V of the Police Act 1997 and was launched in March 2002.

The Crime and Disorder Act 1998

The Crime and Disorder Act 1998 set up the Youth Justice Board (YJB) and youth offender teams and introduced many new measures, including diversionary measures for the police to use with young people involved in less serious offences. These included police reprimands and final warnings and new sentences such as the reparation order and the action plan order.

Dihydrocodeine

Dihydrocodeine is a slightly stronger painkiller than paracetamol, and is known as an opioid.

Drug education counselling and confidential advice (DECCA)

DECCA is a young people's drug service which tackles issues relating to drugs, alcohol and tobacco. It receives referrals from agencies, organisations, professionals, parents, carers and young people themselves. All referred young people are assessed and assigned an appropriate worker, either treatment or education.

Drug treatment and testing orders (DTTO)

Introduced in 2000 as a new community sentence, aimed at breaking the link between drug use and crime. They are now being phased out and replaced by a drug rehabilitation requirement in the community order.

Detention and training order (DTO)

The detention and training order (DTO) is the custodial sentence for 12 to 17-year-olds. Sentences are between four months and two years: the first half of the sentence is spent in custody while the second half is spent in the community under the supervision of the youth offending team (YOT).

Employment, training and education (ETE)

A scheme where probation services work with training services and colleges to equip offenders under supervision with the skills needed to gain employment. They focus on key skills such as literacy and numeracy, and give offenders the opportunity to work towards NVQ awards.

European social fund (ESF)

Established to improve employment opportunities in the European Union and help raise living standards. It aims to help people fulfil their potential by giving them better skills and better job prospects.

FIDO

Fact, Interpretation, Decision, Outcome. A groupwork exercise that explores the relationship between facts and the interpretations that we attach to facts. Y-Pac received training on this technique from the voluntary organisation Leap Confronting Conflict.

Final warning

Introduced by the Crime and Disorder Act 1998 to replace police cautions for young people aged between 10 and 17 years. A second offence will result in a final warning while a third offence, no matter how minor, leads to a criminal charge. Warnings are more serious than reprimands. Young people receiving a final warning are referred to the YOT.

Intensive Supervision and Surveillance Programme (ISSP)

ISSP is a non-custodial intervention available for young offenders, which combines community-based surveillance with a comprehensive and sustained focus on tackling the factors that contribute to the young person's offending behaviour. It targets the most active repeat young offenders and those who commit the most serious crimes. It is a direct alternative to custody. Most young people will spend six months on an ISSP. The intensive period of supervision (25 hours per week) usually lasts for the first three months of the programme. Following this, the supervision continues at a reduced intensity (a minimum of five hours per week, plus weekend support) for a further three months. On completion of the ISSP the young person will continue to be supervised by the youth offending service (YOS) for the remaining period of their order.

Investors in People

The national standard setting out good practice in the training and development of people in order to achieve business goals. The expansion of the standard is a key element of the government's Skills Strategy.

Licence supervision

When a prisoner is released from prison under the supervision of the probation service they must report to a nominated officer on the day of their release. Licence conditions will be explained and times for a series of appointments set out. Conditions may include living in a specific place or staying away from a certain area. Breach can lead to a return to prison.

Multi-agency public protection arrangements (MAPPA)

A risk-management plan that supports the assessment and management of the most serious sexual and violent offenders. It was introduced in 2001 and brings together the police, probation and prison services as the MAPPA Responsible Authority.

Multi-agency public protection panels (MAPPP)

Comprised of senior representatives of local agencies to scrutinise local cases where offenders are deemed to pose the highest risk of causing serious harm or whose management is problematic. The panels have the ability to commit extra resources to support the individual.

National Mentoring Network (NMN)

A membership-based organisation to support the growth of mentoring. It has over 1,600 members.

Neighbourhood Renewal Fund (NRF)

A form of local government finance in England since July 2000. NRF is allocated to multi-agency local strategic partnerships in the 88 local authority areas judged to be the most deprived. It is intended to support social regeneration.

New Deal

A government initiative introduced in 1998 as part of the 'welfare to work' initiative. It offers people who have been unemployed for a long time, opportunities to improve skills and get into employment. It also has schemes to support people into self-employment.

National Offender Management Service (NOMS)

Created in 2004 with the aim of reducing reoffending and protecting the public. NOMS includes a number of organisations, in particular the prison and probation services, and is putting a system in place to deliver end-to-end management of offenders.

Offender Assessment System (OASys)

A system used by both the prison and probation services to determine the issues relating to offending behaviour and appropriate interventions.

Onset assessment tool

A referral and assessment framework that identifies whether a young person would benefit from early interventions. It highlights risk and protective factors in the young person's life. It is primarily used by YJB prevention programmes.

Practical Quality Assurance System for Small Organisations (PQASSO)

A system created by the voluntary sector that helps management to run an organisation effectively and efficiently.

Procurator fiscal

A procurator fiscal is the public prosecutor in Scotland.

Public protection liaison officer (PPLO)

PPLOs help to support and monitor offenders in the community. They help offenders maintain their accommodation in the community; ensure that the conditions and requirements of supervision plans/licences are adhered to and reduce the risk of offending.

Recruitment and Employment Confederation (REC)

The trade body that supports and represents the recruitment industry.

Referral order

Introduced by the Youth Justice Criminal Evidence Act 1999. Used for all young people aged 10 to 17 years who have been convicted of an offence for the first time and a custodial sentence is not imposed. They are referred to a youth offender panel (YOP) for between three and twelve months. See below for what the YOP does.

Rehabilitation of Offenders Act (ROA) 1974

The Rehabilitation of Offenders Act 1974 enables some criminal convictions to become 'spent', or ignored, after a 'rehabilitation period'. A rehabilitation period is a set length of time from the date of conviction. After this period, with certain exceptions, an ex-offender is not normally obliged to mention their conviction when applying for a job or obtaining insurance, or when involved in criminal or civil proceedings.

The length of the rehabilitation period depends on the sentence given, not the offence committed. For a custodial sentence, the length of time actually served is irrelevant; the rehabilitation period is decided by the original sentence. Custodial sentences of more than 2.5 years can never become spent.

Reparation

The act of trying to repair the harm done. It may take many forms, including the payment of money as compensation to the victim; work for the victim; or community reparation/payback.

Sex offender treatment programme (SOTP)

Attendance on a SOTP is ordered by the court. Following assessment by probation, a programme of individual or group sessions will be devised to encourage self-control mechanisms to change attitudes and behaviour and stop further offending.

Sheriff courts

The local court service in Scotland.

Supervision order

A sentence for young people aged 10 to 17 years which was introduced by the Crime and Disorder Act 1998. It can last for up to three years and can have conditions attached, specified activities, that can last for up to 90 days. Examples of 'specified activities' might be participation in an ISSP, drug treatment (for young people aged 16+ years), curfews, or residence requirements. YOTs may also require the young person to take part in activities that are not specified by the court, reparation schemes and anger management courses.

Supporting People Programme

Offers vulnerable people the opportunity to improve their quality of life by providing a stable environment, and greater independence. It will deliver high-quality and strategically planned housing-related services, which are cost-effective and reliable, and complement existing care services. The planning and development of services will be needs led. Supporting People is a working partnership of local government, service users and support agencies.

Universal Monitoring & Information System package (UMIS)

UMIS enables its users across a whole range of agencies including health, social services, education and voluntary sectors to share data and therefore monitor, co-ordinate and evaluate all areas of work responsibility for a particular case. This new approach allows UMIS users to assess a complex case with many disparate details rapidly so as to anticipate and, where necessary, intervene earlier in order to prevent young people offending.

Unpaid work requirement

One of the 12 requirements in the community order introduced in the Criminal Justice Act 2003. Sentencers can order between 40 and 300 hours of work to be completed within 12 months. The work is supervised by the probation service.

Youth Justice Board (YJB)

Established by the Crime and Disorder Act 1998 to oversee the implementation of the youth justice reforms, and advise on the prevention of reoffending.

Youth offender panel (YOP)

A panel consists of two volunteers recruited directly from the local community alongside a YOT member. They talk to the young person, their parents and (where possible) the victim of the crime, to agree a tailor-made contract aimed at putting things right. The contract might include a letter of apology to the victim, removing graffiti, or cleaning up estates and communities. It will also include activities to prevent further offending, such as getting young people back into school and help with alcohol or drug misuse.

Youth offending team (YOT)

YOTs were set up under the Crime and Disorder Act 1998. They are multi-agency teams, which draw their members from probation, social services, local education authorities, health authorities and the police. The multi-agency approach is designed to ensure consistency and sharing of information between statutory and other agencies involved in preventing crime and rehabilitating young offenders.

References

Barton, A. and Teagle, R. (2004) An Evaluation of the White Gold Project, Plymouth: University of Plymouth.

Carter, C., (2007) Offenders and Nature: Helping People - Helping Nature. Farnham: Forest Research (12pp). http://www.forestresearch.gov.uk/pdf/offenders_and_Nature_Report.pdf/$FILE/Offenders_and_Nature_Report.pdf

Carter, Lord (2007) Securing the Future: Proposals for the Efficient and Sustainable Use of Custody in England and Wales, www.justice.gov.uk/docs/securing-the-future.htm

Clancy, A., Lane, J., Morgan, B. and Maguire, M. (2004) Moving Forward with Mentoring: An Evaluation of the Transitional Support Scheme in Wales, London: Home Office (RDS), National Assembly for Wales and Cardiff University.

Cutting, E. (2004) The Effectiveness of Sacro's Alcohol Education Probation Programme in Reducing Re-convictions, London: Rethinking Crime and Punishment, Esmée Fairbairn Foundation.

Davidson, S. and Whyte, K. (2007) Domestic Abuse in Scotland: Findings from the 2003 and 2004 Scottish Crime Surveys, Edinburgh: Scottish Executive Social Research.

Department of Justice (2004) Reducing Reoffending: National Action Plan, London: Home Office.

Fletcher, D., Woodhill, D. and Herrington, A. (1998)
Building Bridges into Employment and Training for Ex-Offenders, York: The Joseph Rowntree Foundation.

The Howard League for Penal Reform (2006) Out for Good: The Resettlement Needs of Young Men in Prison, London: the Howard League for Penal Reform.

The Howard League for Penal Reform (2007)
Community Sentences Bulletin 1: Adults and Community Sentences, London: the Howard League for Penal Reform.

Nacro (2005) Integrated Resettlement: Putting the Pieces Together, London: Nacro.

Quaker Peace and Social Witness (2005) Circles of Support and Accountability: The First Three Years, April 2002 to March 2005, London: Quaker Communications.

Reed, C.A. (2004) Staffordshire's Intensive Floating Support Scheme for High Risk Offenders: Initial Evaluation, PLACE: C.A Reed Management and Consultancy.

Research and Evaluation Services (2004) Synopsis of Evaluation of IMPACT: 1st October 2001 to 31st March 2004. Final Report 1st October 2004, Belfast: Research and Evaluation Services.

Research and Evaluation Services (2005) Synopsis of Evaluation of IMPACT Project: 1st April 2004 to 31st March 2005. Final Report 4th October 2005, Belfast: Research and Evaluation Services.

Rethinking Crime and Punishment (2004) Rethinking Crime and Punishment: The Report, Esmee Fairnbairn Foundation, London

Sacro (2006) Evaluation Report on Sacro's Alcohol Education Probation Programme April 2006, Edinburgh: Sacro.

Sacro (2007a) Evaluation Report on Sacro's Another Way Service, April 2007, Edinburgh: Sacro.

Sacro (2007b) Sacro Domestic Abuse Group (DAG) and Associated Services – Evaluation Report 2007, Edinburgh: Sacro.

Shapland, J., Atkinson, A., Colledge, E., Dignan, J., Howes, M., Johnstone, J., Pennant, R., Robinson, G. and Sorsby, A. (2004) Implementing Restorative Justice Schemes (Crime Reduction Programme): A Report on the First Year, Sheffield: Institute for the Study of the Legal Profession, University of Sheffield.

Shapland, J., Atkinson, A., Atkinson, H., Chapman, B., Colledge, E., Dignan, J., Howes, M., Johnstone, J., Robinson, G. and Sorsby, A. (2006) Restorative Justice in Practice: The Second Report from the Evaluation of Three Schemes, Sheffield: Centre for Criminological Research, University of Sheffield.

Sherman, L.W. and Strang, H. (2007) Restorative Justice: The Evidence, London: The Smith Institute.

Southern, R., Annison, J. Fisher, A., Vicente, F., and Farbus, L. (2007) Evaluation of the Warbarth Project in Cornwall, Social Research and Regeneration Unit, University of Plymouth.

Youth Justice Board (2005) Risk and Protective Factors, London: Youth Justice Board.

Mission Statement

The Howard League for Penal Reform wants a safe society where fewer people are victims of crime.

The Howard League for Penal Reform believes that offenders must make amends for what they have done and change their lives.

The Howard League for Penal Reform believes that community sentences make a person take responsibility and live a law-abiding life in the community.